DATE DUE

OCT 29 2010			
MAR 25 2011			
NOV 29 2012			

Demco, Inc. 38-293

At Issue

Islamic Fundamentalism

Other Books in the At Issue Series:

At Issue

Islamic Fundamentalism

David M. Haugen, Book Editor

GREENHAVEN PRESS
A part of Gale, Cengage Learning

GALE
CENGAGE Learning˙

Detroit • New York • San Francisco • New Haven, Conn • Waterville, Maine • London

GALE
CENGAGE Learning™

Christine Nasso, *Publisher*
Elizabeth Des Chenes, *Managing Editor*

© 2008 Greenhaven Press, a part of Gale, Cengage Learning.

For more information, contact:
Greenhaven Press
27500 Drake Rd.
Farmington Hills, MI 48331-3535
Or you can visit our Internet site at gale.cengage.com

LIBRARY OF CONGRESS CATALOGING-IN-PUBLICATION DATA

Islamic fundamentalism / David M. Haugen, book editor.
    p. cm. -- (At issue)
    Includes bibliographical references and index.
    ISBN-13: 978-0-7377-3689-2 (hardcover)
    ISBN-10: 0-7377-3689-5 (hardcover)
    ISBN-13: 978-0-7377-3690-8 (pbk.)
    ISBN-10: 0-7377-3690-9 (pbk.)
    1. Islamic fundamentalism. 2. Islam--Essence, genius, nature. 3. Islam--Relations. 4. Islam and world politics. 5. Islamic countries--Relations--United States. 6. Uni-ted States--Relations--Islamic countries. 7. Islam--21st century. I. Haugen, David M., 1969-
    BP166.14.F85I85 2008
    297.09--dc22
                                                                    2007029302

Printed in the United States of America
2 3 4 5 6 7 12 11 10 09 08

Contents

Introduction

Islamic fundamentalism has become a catchphrase in the Western world for Muslim ideology that is bent on shaping the world around religious scripture as revealed primarily in the Muslim holy book, the Qur'an. Some in the West fear Islamic fundamentalism because media commentators and political pundits often portray it as restricting personal freedoms (especially those of women) and standing in opposition to secular interests (such as capitalism) that have made Western nations influential in world affairs. Others disparage Islamic fundamentalism as a form of fanaticism that seeks to convert all nations to Muslim law, often through aggression and violence aimed at infidels who cherish a more secularized global order. Yet while these fears have been exacerbated in light of the September 11, 2001, terrorist attacks on the United States and the subsequent wars in Afghanistan and Iraq, the phrase itself has lost its currency. Indeed, the United States and its allies have found the term troublesome in defining a seemingly anti-Western philosophy that has more than just religious idealism as its driving force in the Muslim world.

Those who prefer to discontinue the use of the phrase "Islamic fundamentalism" to denote the Muslim factions that paint the United States and other Western powers as the foes of Islam contend that there is nothing inherent in a fundamentalist view of Muslim scripture that calls for such enmity. Writing in the *National Catholic Reporter*, Margot Patterson asserts that "most Islamic fundamentalists have much in common with their Christian counterparts, both perceiving reality through an interpretation of scripture that they view as inerrant." Thus, fundamentalist views are not necessarily anti-Western, and many who were critical of growing Muslim militancy understandably wished to stop connecting violence with religion. President George W. Bush has been one of the most careful in choosing terminology that separates the United States' enemies from the vast Islamic populations of the world. In January 2002, while speaking in California, the president made clear that the War on Terror, the U.S. reaction to the September 2001 attacks, was directed only at those that seek to harm the United States or any nation that preserves freedom. "We're taking action against evil people," he declared, "Because this great nation of many religions understands, our war is not against Islam, or against faith practiced by the Muslim people. Our war is a war against evil."

Three years later, during a speech before the National Endowment for Democracy, President Bush found new ways to refer to the ideology of America's Muslim enemies without condemning Islam. Carefully evading a predilection for loaded terminology other than the consistent use of "radicals" and "terrorists," the president said, "Some call this evil Islamic radicalism; others, militant Jihadism; still others, Islamo-fascism. Whatever it's called, this ideology is very different from the religion of Islam. This form of radicalism exploits Islam to serve a violent, political vision: the establishment, by terrorism and subversion and insurgency, of a totalitarian empire that denies all political and religious freedom." By the following year, Bush had shown a clear preference for the term "Islamo-fascism," which he said "comes in different forms. They [the Islamo-fascists] share the same tactics, which is to destroy people and things in order to create chaos in the hopes that their vision of the world become predominant in the Middle East."

The term Islamo-fascism has become popular with the White House and other proponents of the war against terrorism and its political motivations. Author Roger Scruton claims that the word has caught on "not least because it provides a convenient way of announcing that you are not against Islam but only against its perversion by the terrorists. But this prompts the question whether terrorism is really as alien to

Islam as we should all like to believe." In a 2006 article for the Ignatius Insight Web site, an outlet for Catholic views on world events, Father James V. Schall answers Scruton's query by pointing out that terrorists, like those that committed the September 11 tragedies and subsequent murders, went to their deaths willingly, not for some fascistic government but because "they were doing the work of Allah. The world could not know peace until it was subjugated to his rule as laid down in the holy book." Other critics have avoided the religious dimension but still ridiculed the term as inappropriate and politically motivated. Katha Pollitt argues in one of her articles on Islamo-fascism for the *Nation* that the concept of fascism is allied with nationalist, secular movements that dream of building powerful modernized states. In her opinion it has little to do with disparate interest groups in Muslim countries that are often stateless and driven by religious conviction and vengeance against Western domination. She states that Islamo-fascism is an "emotional" term that intends to present "the bewildering politics of the Muslim world as a simple matter of Us versus Them, with war to the end the only answer, as with [German dictator Adolf] Hitler."

Hoping not to be mired in the political and historical complexity of marrying Islam and fascism, a majority of today's journalists and writers have turned to the terms radical Islam or Islamism to capture the non-specific brand of extremism that uses Islam to promote a political agenda. These blanket terms provide enough room to house the anti-Western, anti-democracy philosophies of terrorist organizations like al-Qaeda (the perpetrators of the September 11 attacks and many terrorist acts since the 1990s), the Wahhabi sect of Saudi Arabia (which has such a strict view of Islamic scripture that it has declared itself opposed to moderate Muslims who show any sign of straying from religious purity), as well as pro-democracy populist movements such as Hamas (the Islamist party in Palestine that currently holds a majority in the Palestinain National Authority). Western writers also employ the phrase "political Islam" to describe this all-encompassing extremism, because within it, the political and religious aims of Islam coalesce. Therefore, Islamists are depicted as believing that the Muslim community has strayed too far from the fundamentals of Islamic law and that part of this erring has been caused by the corrupting influence of Western secularism. Only by returning society to the true path of Islam can the problems of the Muslim world be rectified. Islamic authorities often refute this categorization, maintaining that the term Islamism is just a way for Western politicians to create a false dichotomy between supposedly "good" Muslims and radical troublemakers. Many Islamists assert that their views are in line with the majority of Muslim people and not some violent, politically motivated fanaticism.

Providing a name for Muslim extremism indicates, to some extent, how Westerners respond to it. Calling it Islamo-fascism, for example, implies that the United States and its allies are justified in carrying out a war against an enemy that is, in the words of former Speaker of the House Newt Gingrich, "prepared to use the power of the state to impose a totalitarian system on others." Taking issue with that term may signify that one believes the enemy is not a totalitarian entity that can be defeated ideologically. Other labels are equally controversial. Referring to this brand of radicalism as Islamism, political Islam, or Islamic fundamentalism leads to arguments about whether religion is to blame for the destructive acts committed in its name. The authors represented in *At Issue: Islamic Fundamentalism* ascribe various names to Muslim extremism. Each seems keenly aware that labeling this phenomenon entails a specific course that the West should follow in managing what has proven detrimental to global security. All acknowledge, though, that the continuing threat of fundamentalist Islam or its political arm has as much to do with U.S. foreign policy as it does with Muslim religious or secular goals.

1

Defining Islamism and Jihad

Pippi Van Slooten

Pippi Van Slooten is a doctoral student in political science at the University of Nebraska, Lincoln. She is a former soldier who served as part of the U.S. Army Reserves during Operation Iraqi Freedom.

Islam is a religion that has always had a political dimension. Throughout recent history, political Islam, or Islamism, has defined itself through opposition to the encroachment of Western influences in Arab lands. Islamic fundamentalists have embraced more conservative views as the West has spread its business practices and cultural exports throughout Islamic states. The fundamentalist trend has become infused in the politics of Islam as more adherents see Western influence as a weakening of the Muslim political and religious community. To counter the deterioration, some Islamic leaders have emphasized jihad, *a holy war in defense of Islam. Some view* jihad *as a struggle to convert unbelievers. While many stress that this process of conversion should be peaceful, the more radical Islamists view* jihad *as a justified contest of arms to stem Western domination and advance the cause of Islam.*

Islam—as a religion, as a cultural force, and as a political movement—had a turbulent beginning when its prophet, Muhammad, fled from Mecca [a holy city in western Saudi Arabia] and established a new Islamic political community (*umma*) at Medina [a holy city 200 hundred miles north of Mecca]. This was accomplished by waging violent and often

Pippi Van Slooten, "Dispelling Myths about Islam and Jihad," *Peace Review*, vol. 17, 2005 pp. 289–94. © 2005 Pippi Van Slooten. Reproduced by permission of Taylor & Francis, Ltd., www.tandf.co.uk/journals and the author.

bloody war, and these beginnings, coupled with the "crusades" by the Western Christians in the "holy land" centuries later, made the sword into the symbolic image of Islam in the West. But the word *islam* is actually closely related to the Arabic word for peace: *salem*. This is because Muslims believe that true peace can only be achieved through a complete obedience to the will of God. The Arabic term *islam* means "submission" and comes from the term *aslama*, which means to surrender or resign oneself. In the religion of Islam, the fundamental duty of each follower is to submit to *Allah* (God) and to do whatever God wants of him. A person who follows Islam is called a Muslim, and this means one who surrenders to God.

A Peaceful Religion

A commitment to *islam* is supposed to result in a constant struggle to achieve peace, justice, and equality. Understanding what the term *islam* means, as well as its cultural connotations for the millions of followers of this fast-growing movement, is helpful in understanding the religion and the political system from which it derives its name. But it is a mistake to assume there are not varied interpretations and standpoints on current Islamic religious and political thought. Although there is an agreement on what certain characteristics of a Muslim government should be—especially in regard to its role and responsibilities to the *umma* (religious/civic community)—there are still varied interpretations of what an Islamic state and society should look like. And, as [political scholar] Hamza Ates has suggested, although the interest on this subject has increased since the September 11, 2001 terror attacks, most of the writings on so-called Islamic terrorism are more sensational and pop-cultural rather than analytical in nature. Thus, in contrast, it's important to instead introduce a few of the peaceful beliefs and political theories of Islam—the fastest growing religious-political movement in the world today.

Reaction to Foreign Domination

Modern political Islam or Islamism was strongly influenced by the social frustrations following the economic crises of the 1970s and 1980s. These cultural revolutions throughout the Middle East produced large groups of young intellectual Muslims who were college educated and often wealthy, but who could not easily find opportunities or outlets to satisfy the aspirations that had been inflamed in them by their nationalist governments.

Islamism is a belief in creating a particular order based around the religious and ethical worldview of Islam.

[Sociology professor] Bryan Turner has identified four periods of Islamic political action in response to the social and cultural crises caused by foreign domination and internal struggle: First, in the nineteenth century, early reformist movements throughout the Middle East and North Africa critically attacked foreign political and military domination of their region and were labeled "fundamentalist," due to their belief in a "pristine" Islam of the early community of the Prophet. The second period of activism occurred in the 1970s with the rise of the Muslim Brotherhood in Egypt, with its fundamentalist views and its insistence on the blending of religion and state through Islam. The third period began in the aftermath of the Arab defeat in the 1967 war with Israel and reached a high point with the Iranian Revolution in 1979, continuing with the pan-Arab opposition to the Russian invasion of Afghanistan. And the fourth (current) period of Islamist resistance began with the Gulf War in 1990 and with the stationing of U.S. troops around Muslim holy sites in Saudi Arabia. The resentment simmering during this period finally boiled over into the September 11 terror attacks by the radical Islamist organization, Al Qaeda.

The decade of the 1980s was marked by the rise of ultra-conservative and politically active Islamic movements throughout much of the Arab world. These movements (labeled "fundamentalist" in Western media) sought the government institutionalization of Islamic law and social principles. The Ayatollah Khomeini called for an overthrow of the house of Saud in Saudi Arabia as a direct challenge to the legitimacy of the monarchy as custodian of the holy sites of Islam. This challenge would intensify after the monarchy's decision, years later, to allow U.S. troops to be stationed on their soil during the first Gulf War.

Wahhabiism and Conformity to the True Faith

Many of the September 11 attackers, as well as their spiritual leader Osama bin Laden, not only lived in Saudi Arabia, but also were followers of a radical Islamic political sect that began in central Arabia in the mid-eighteenth century. Wahhabiism, commonly known as the Wahhabi movement, grew out of the preaching of Muhammad ibn Abd al Wahhab, an Islamic legal scholar who preached the message of Islamic reform. He was concerned by what he viewed as a laxness in adhering to Islamic law and in performing religious devotions. But in what would seem contrary to the radical views of his modern, more violent, followers, Wahhab was also opposed to what he perceived to be an indifference to the plight of widows and orphans and a failure to allocate shares of inheritance fairly to women. The modern Wahhabi emphasis on conformity is based on a belief that external appearance and behavior is a visible expression of inward faith. So, when one conforms in dress, in prayer or in other activities publicly, this becomes a statement of being a true Muslim—even though these activities are not necessarily expressly called for in the Qu'ran. In this sense, public opinion becomes a regulator of individual behavior, and it becomes the responsibility of each

Muslim to look after the behavior of his neighbors and to admonish them if they go astray.

No Separation between Church and State

Against this historical and cultural context, Islamism is a belief in creating a particular order based around the religious and ethical worldview of Islam. An "Islamist" is one dedicated to seeing this political order become a major global force, whereas in contrast, a "Muslim" is one who submits to the beliefs codified in the Qu'ran and in the *sunna* (the practices of Muhammad). Although Western political theorists argue that modern Islamists are basically reacting to and rearticulating Western ideas, such as theories on hegemony, international relations, and even on human rights, Medieval Islamist theorists such as Ibn Khaldun, Ibm Rushd, and Ibn Zafar confronted these ideas long before they were contemplated in the West. Ibn Zafar's twelfth century writings on power and leadership, for example, actually predate his far more often cited Western counterpart: Machiavelli. Long before *The Prince*, Ibn Zafar wrote *Sulwan al Muta*, which was also written as advice to rulers, and which offered an empirical analysis of power as well as a set of maxims and strategies to be used by a virtuous ruler to preserve his power and secure his holdings.

[M]ost Muslims are united in their belief in the Qu'ran and in their ethical views—particularly in terms of war and peace.

Christians often cite Jesus' admonition to "render unto Caesar what is Caesar's and unto God what is God's" as an early justification for the separation of church and state in the role of civil affairs, in effect creating two separate spheres of moral, ethical, and political responsibility for the individual and for society. But this is not the case in Islam. The Prophet Muhammad did not simply found a religious movement: he began a political and social community grounded in a shared faith, an *umma*. He was the arbiter, judge, military commander, and political leader, as well as spiritual guide for this community. Because Muhammad received and reported revelations directly from God, he was the legislator for the community as well. Muhammad was thus replacing tribal and familial loyalty with a larger loyalty that was new to this community.

But when Muhammad died, that was the end of the revelations from God. Many of the sects became embroiled in turmoil, resulting from the search for a spiritual and political successor. The Sunnis are Muslims who are considered the more "orthodox" believers. Sunnis follow all of the most traditional beliefs and actions. The Shi'a take their name from a shortened form of Shi'at Ali, which means the party of Ali. They are a sect that split over a belief that Ali, Muhammad's first cousin and husband to the Prophet's favorite daughter, Fatima, deserved to be the first successor to Muhammad. But Muhammad's family and supporters were behind Aisha, Muhammad's wife. Ali's forces defeated Aisha's at the Battle of the Camel in 656, after which she apologized and was allowed to return to her home in Medina, where she left public life. Along with the Wahhabi, there are smaller sects such as the Sufi, the Kahrijites, and the Ismailis, but the Sunnis are the largest sect of all (representing the vast majority of Muslims), and the Shi'ites are the largest minority (except in Iran where they are the majority). But overall, most Muslims are united in their belief in the Qu'ran and in their ethical views—particularly in terms of war and peace.

War against the Unenlightened

Islam is a system of moral obligations deriving from a belief in divine revelation and based on the belief that human knowledge can never be adequate or complete compared to that which is revealed by God. This is important when trying to understand the concept of *jihad* as a religious imperative.

Believers must act on the basis of Allah's knowledge (which is greater and more complete than man's knowledge), and to act on human knowledge alone is to act on ignorance. The exclusive source of knowledge and truth for Muslims is God. Ethical action, even in war, always relates to actions revealed by God in the Qu'ran. This view is shared by all Muslim sects. Most modern debate among Muslims about the Islamic ethics of war and peace is based on literal readings of the Qu'ranic verses pertaining to Muhammad's actions in early Medina. Quotes from the Qu'ran serve as discussion points on war and peace. The common foundation for all Islamic concepts of war and peace is a worldview based on the distinction between *dar al islam* and *dar al harb*.

[In Islam,] any war against the unenlightened is morally justified in order to free the souls of the people trapped by a government not guided by God.

In Islam, peace requires that non-Muslims submit to the call of Islam, either by converting to it or by accepting the status of a religious minority (*dhimmi*) and paying the imposed poll tax for security. World peace, then, is reached only with the conversion or submission of all humankind to Islam. Unbelievers are blamed for the state of war. So, *dar al harb* is a state of nature where [English philosopher Thomas] Hobbes' war of all against all is possible due to a lack of enlightenment through Islam, and *dar al islam* is a state of peace where man's will and knowledge is set aside for a more enlightened worldview. Understanding this distinction is important for understanding what the Western media (and Islamist radicals) have often translated as a battle between "believers" and "infidels." It is also relevant to understanding the nature of *jihad* as a metaphorical war against ignorance rather than as religious Armageddon.

Popular perceptions are powerful and can often be manipulated to achieve short-term political goals: this is true for Islamist cultures as well as for the West. Historically, the establishment of the *umma* at Medina and the spread of this new religion by Muhammad were accompanied by violent, bloody warfare. Thus, the sword became the symbolic image of Islam in the West. But for Islamists, the rise of the West as a superior military power led to the globalization of the European model of the modern political state. This posed a major challenge for the dichotomy between *dar al islam* and *dar al harb* in a world of competing, secular states. What, then, causes war? What can bring peace—from an Islamist perspective?

Two Views on War and Peace

The Western distinction between just and unjust war is unknown in Islam: this is because any war against the unenlightened is morally justified in order to free the souls of the people trapped by a government not guided by God. Similarly, when the unenlightened attack Muslims, it is an unjust act of war. Islam recognizes moral constraints on the conduct of military actions during war, but sometimes extreme measures are necessary and forbidden acts are carried out to free the people.

Jihad *is regarded by some as Islam's instrument for carrying out its ultimate objective of turning all people into enlightened believers and thus bringing about a more peaceful world.*

According to Islamic scholars [Sohai] Hashmi and [Bassam] Tibi, there are two dominant Islamist perspectives on war and peace at work in modern Middle Eastern politics: conformist and fundamentalist. Conformists seek to conform Islamic views to a dominant non-Islamic world. Modern Muslim conformist leaders are characterized not by a submission to God, but by a submission to international standards of law and by a general acceptance of peaceful relations with non-Islamic countries.

The reasoning behind the conformist view is that Islamic states are weak when compared militarily, economically, and culturally to non-Muslim states, and must therefore conform in order to survive. But even among conformists, the belief that true peace is only possible among Muslim states persists. The difference is that moderate and conformist Muslims use this reasoning to re-interpret *jihad* to discourage the use of force. It is an intellectual debate, not the end of world conflict.

Fundamentalists, on the other hand, use the power difference internationally between Muslim and non-Muslim states as a justification for a warlike interpretation of jihad. But in line with Islamic tradition, they do not mention "states." What is at issue is the Islamic community as a whole against the rest of the unenlightened world. Islamic fundamentalism as a movement dates back to the 1970s, although its intellectual and organizational roots can be traced back to 1928, when the Muslim Brotherhood was founded in Egypt. Fundamentalists apply the word *jihad* indiscriminately against non-Muslims and "secular" Muslim states alike. In the end, both groups hope their side's war to be just (*jihad*).

The Politics of *Jihad*

Much of the controversy today surrounding the concept of *jihad* emerges from the tensions between its legal and ethical dimensions—is it a juristic or moral act? *Jihad* is regarded by some as Islam's instrument for carrying out its ultimate objective of turning all people into enlightened believers and thus bringing about a more peaceful world. The classical religious doctrine of Islam explains war in two ways: first, as *qital*, or armed conflict, which is a last resort under Islam and is a war of self-defense, and second, as *jihad*, or a permanent irreconcilable moral condition between Muslims and non-Muslims.

But the Qu'ran states that Muslims must not be the aggressors. Through overuse, and at times deliberate misuse to further political agendas, the concept of *jihad* has become confused with the related Islamic concept of *qital*. But the Qu'ran, to most Islamic scholars, seems to advocate *jihad* as a more persuasive effort to enlighten a group through reasoned argument—not through violent conflict or terrorist acts. But just as their Christian or secular counterparts in the West, Muslim leaders tend to quote the Qu'ran selectively to support their own ethical and political views.

This practice has confused the meaning of jihad, and the current debate about the term dates back to the rise of political Islam and the division of the religion of Muhammad into warring factions. But *salem* ultimately means peace, and both Muslims and non-Muslims alike should do more to understand the peaceful foundations of the religious and political beliefs within the larger culture of Islam.

Islam is an international political movement, as well as one of the fastest growing religious movements in the world. But although it has a lingering image in the West that is associated with the sword, it also embodies a series of beliefs on how war is to be both conducted and also avoided.

2

Islamism Is a Reaction against Secularism

Dinesh D'Souza

A former senior policy analyst under the Ronald Reagan administration, Dinesh D'Souza is an expert in international affairs and U.S. policy. He is currently a fellow at the Hoover Institution at Stanford University. He is the author of several books including The Enemy at Home: The Cultural Left and Its Responsibility for 9/11.

Islamic radicals are not standing up to the United States and its Western allies because they fear the spread of Christianity into Muslim lands. Islam has traditionally tolerated other monotheistic religions. Instead, Islamists believe the West has lost its religious convictions and has embraced a secularist perspective. Islamic fundamentalists, therefore, are motivated to counter the influence of Western secularism that has been foisted upon Muslim people through cultural exports and political manipulation.

For many Western liberals—and even some conservatives—the war on terror is a clash of opposed fundamentalisms: Christian fundamentalism vs. Islamic fundamentalism. So, in this view, Christian and Muslim religious fanatics are once again fighting each other, as they have done in the past.

From this perspective, the best solution is for America to stand up for the principles of secularism and oppose both Muslim fundamentalism and Christian fundamentalism. But in reality secularism is not the solution. Secularism is the

Dinesh D'Souza, "Secularism Is Not the Solution," *Townhall.com*, February 19, 2007. Reproduced by permission.

problem. It is the West's agenda of secularism that is alienating traditional Muslims and pushing them toward the radical camp.

➤ The common understanding of the battle as one between two rival fundamentalisms is superficially supported by [terrorist leader Osama] Bin Laden's rhetoric declaring a religious war of civilizations. Bin Laden speaks of the world being divided into the "region of faith" and the "region of infidelity." At times Bin Laden defines the clash as one between the Muslims and the crusaders.

But the context of Bin Laden's arguments clearly shows that Bin Laden is not speaking of a religious war between Islam and Christianity. In the same videotaped remarks where Bin Laden posits these conflicts, he praises Christianity. In one statement Bin Laden observes that Islam respects the prophets of Judaism, Christianity and Islam "without distinguishing among them."

Islamic radicals . . . make their case against America and the West on the grounds that these cultures have abandoned Christianity.

Respect for Christians and Jesus

In the classical Muslim understanding, there is a fundamental distinction between Jews and Christians on the one hand and polytheists and atheists on the other. According to Islam, Judaism and Christianity are incomplete but genuine revelations. As monotheists, Jews and Christians have historically been entitled to Muslim respect and even protection. In every Islamic empire, from the Umayyad to the Abbasid to the Ottoman, Jews and Christians were permitted to practice their religion and in no Muslim regime has it ever been considered legitimate to systematically kill them.

By contrast, polytheists and atheists have always been anathema to Islam. The Koran says, "Fight the pagans all together as they fight you all together" and "Slay the idolaters wherever you find them." These passages, which Bin Laden frequently quotes, do not refer to Christians, because Christians are not considered pagans or idolaters. Rather, they refer to those, like the Beduins of ancient Arabia, who worship many gods or no god. Muslims are commanded to fight these unbelievers, especially when they threaten the House of Islam.

Muslim radicals could repudiate the entire Islamic tradition and argue that Christians and Jews are no different from atheists and deserve the same treatment. But this claim would undoubtedly alienate traditional Muslims. Sheikh Muhammad Tantawi, head of Al Azhar University, recently argued the traditional view that "Islam has never been and will never be at war with Christianity." For Bin Laden to declare war against Christianity would even divide the radical Muslim camp. The influential radical sheikh Yusuf Qaradawi has said that as Muslims, "We believe in the Jewish and Christian scriptures. Our Islamic faith is not complete without them."

America Has Abandoned Christianity

Islamic radicals like Bin Laden make their case against America and the West on the grounds that these cultures have abandoned Christianity. In his May 2006 letter to President [George W.] Bush, [Iranian president Mahmoud] Ahmadinejad faulted America not for being Christian, but for not being Christian enough. Many years earlier, the radical theoretician Sayyid Qutb made the same point. The main reason for the West's moral decay, Qutb argued, is that in the modern era "religious convictions are no more than a matter of antiquarian interest."

Other Muslim radicals today echo these arguments. The influential Pakistani scholar Khurshid Ahmad, leader of the Jamaat-i-Islami, argues, "Had Western culture been based on

Christianity, on morality, on faith, the language and modus operandi of the contact and conflict would have been different. But that is not the case. The choice is between the divine principle and a secular materialistic culture."

 Even though Christianity has eroded, Muslim radicals contend that the ancient crusading spirit now infuses the pagan culture of the West. When Bin Laden calls America a crusader state, he means that America is on a vicious international campaign to impose its atheist system of government and its pagan values on Muslims. How? By supporting secular dictators in Pakistan, Jordan, Egypt and Saudi Arabia. And by exporting a secular culture that undermines the traditional values of Islam.

In this way, Bin Laden argues that America is hell-bent on destroying the Muslim religion. The rallying cry of Islamic radicalism is that "Islam is under attack." In his 1998 declaration Bin Laden called on Muslims to "launch attacks against the armies of the American devils" and to kill Americans whom he identified as the "helpers of Satan." In a 2003 sermon, Bin Laden praised the September 11 hijackers and compared the twin towers of the World Trade Center to the idols in the Kaaba that the Prophet Muhammad destroyed in the year 630 upon his victorious return to Mecca.

Thus the doctrine that the war against terrorism is a battle of two opposed forms of religious fundamentalism is false. This is not why the Islamic radicals are fighting against America. From the perspective of Bin Laden and his allies, the war is between the Muslim-led forces of monotheism and morality against the America-led forces of atheism and immorality. Secularism, not Christian fundamentalism, is responsible for producing a blowback of Muslim rage.

3

Institutionalized Christianity in the West Incites the Growth of Islamism

Richard Alba and Nancy Foner

Richard Alba is a professor of sociology and public policy at the State University of New York in Albany. He is an author and co-author of several books including Remaking the American Mainstream: Assimilation and Contemporary Immigration. *Nancy Foner is a professor of sociology at Hunter College and at the City University of New York Graduate Center. She is an author and editor of several works including* In a New Land: A Comparative View of Immigration.

In Europe, the close affiliation between Church and State has left many non-Christian citizens feeling isolated from their adopted countries. The estrangement often pushes younger generations of European Muslims to embrace Islamic fundamentalism as a means of establishing an identity apart from the institutions that seemingly reject them. In the United States, the separation of Church and State is more rigidly enforced, and the government must safeguard this valuable asset to its liberal policies of ethnic integration.

A s political and religious leaders in this country challenge the longstanding separation between church and state, Americans need only look to Europe, with its anxieties about homegrown Muslim terrorists, for a wake-up call. The Euro-

Richard Alba and Nancy Foner, "Can It Happen Here?" *Nation*, vol. 281, October 17, 2005, pp. 20–21. Copyright © 2005 by The Nation Magazine/The Nation Company, Inc. Reproduced by permission.

pean experience teaches that there is no way for government to favor religion in general; it will favor specific expressions of religion, invariably Christian, and thereby push others aside. In the contemporary, globalized world, where the United States and Western Europe provide new homes to millions of immigrants from all over the world, breaching the wall between religions and government runs great risks.

Yet that appears to be the direction in which we are heading. [In] June [2005] the Supreme Court ruled that the display of a biblical text, the Ten Commandments, on a government monument is not inherently unconstitutional. President [George W.] Bush recently suggested that the theory of intelligent design should be taught in the nation's public schools on an equal basis with the theory of evolution, thereby supporting the demands of some of his most conservative Christian supporters. FEMA [Federal Emergency Management Agency] has just announced that taxpayer money will reimburse religious organizations for their aid to hurricane victims; the Bush Administration has enabled them to receive other direct government funding, which amounted to $2 billion in fiscal year 2004. In the background lurk a host of other specters, such as school vouchers, supported by Bush and the Republican Party, to provide state financial support for religious schools; and the vulnerability of *Roe v. Wade* [the Supreme Court decision that legalizes abortion], which many conservative Christians hope will be overturned by a reconstituted Supreme Court.

Europe's Support of Christianity

In Europe we can see the dangers of the interpenetration of church and state. As secular as Europeans are, their societies have deeply institutionalized religious identities, which are the result of historic settlements after centuries of religious conflict. In France, where *laïcité*, the exclusion of religion from the affairs of state, is the official ideology, the state in fact owns and maintains most Christian churches and allows them to be used for regular religious services. The same law that establishes state possession of religious edifices also prevents the state from building new ones, thus keeping the country's 4-5 million Muslims from enjoying the same privileges as Christians. Most French mosques are, as a consequence, ad hoc structures, not very different from storefront churches. Adding to the religious divide is that half the country's ten or so state-designated national holidays are Catholic in origin; no Muslim holiday has equivalent recognition.

[T]he aggrieved sense of exclusion felt by many Muslims who have grown up in Europe created a huge pool of potential recruits for fundamentalist movements.

In Britain and France the state provides financial support for religious schools as long as they teach the national secular curriculum. Inevitably, these arrangements, while seemingly fair to all religions, favor the most established ones. In Britain (where, incidentally, senior Anglican bishops sit in the House of Lords by right as part of the Anglican "establishment") the government funds nearly 7,000 Church of England and Catholic schools but only five Islamic schools in a nation of 1.6 million Muslims. In the Netherlands the majority of children go to state-supported religious schools, nearly all Protestant and Catholic, while the country's estimated 1 million Muslims have only about thirty-five of their own publicly funded primary schools.

No Room for Muslims

The institutionalization of Christianity in Europe has played a role in the growth of Islamic fundamentalism, for it adds substantially to the barriers confronting second-generation Muslims trying to make their place in European societies. Young people born and raised in the West are not satisfied with the humble positions of their immigrant parents. Yet at the same time, because of the burdens of lower-class origins and racial, ethnic and religious discrimination, the children of Muslim immigrants generally do not have the same opportunities for educational and professional achievement as do those from the European majorities. This situation leads many to resort to Islam as a way of claiming dignity. But Islam cannot solve their dilemma. On the one hand, they confront secular Europeans who are suspicious of claims based on religious beliefs and, on the other, societal institutions and national identities anchored in Christianity that do not make room for Islam.

In the aftermath of the London bombings [in July 2005], we heard that the aggrieved sense of exclusion felt by many Muslims who have grown up in Europe created a huge pool of potential recruits for fundamentalist movements. Certainly, what the homegrown London bombers did requires a deep sense of exclusion: To attack one's own society implies that one cannot imagine oneself as a full-fledged member of it. This sense of exclusion is not simply a matter of poverty or ethnic origin; the interlacing of state and Christianity plays a critical role too.

America Needs Church-State Separation

There was a time when the United States might have headed in the same direction. A century ago Protestant versions of Christianity were more or less "established," in that they dominated the public square, crowding out Catholicism and Judaism, both associated with immigrant populations. But because the state did not officially support or sponsor Protestantism, the newer religions were able over time to achieve parity. This rise in their status helped the descendants of immigrants to enter the mainstream and feel themselves to be fully American. We are now in a new era of immigration, which has brought to this country many adherents of religions outside the Judeo-Christian sphere—Hindus, Muslims and Buddhists among them. If the state now privileges Christian expressions of morality and belief above others, then the successful inclusion of these immigrants and their children will be in peril.

When states do not officially support religions, the only recognition they can offer is symbolic, which is easily extended to all religions. After September 11 George Bush reached out to Muslims, and this was understood as a unifying gesture. But if the United States were to go the way of Europe, such statements would be seen as rhetorical half-measures, undermined by durable inequities. The lessons of Europe's difficulties in integrating its Muslim population are clear. The U.S. legacy of church-state separation has contributed mightily to our success in converting the children of immigrants into patriotic Americans. This is hardly the moment to abandon it.

4

The United States Misunderstands the Appeal of Islamism

Margot Patterson

Margot Patterson is a senior staff writer for the National Catholic Reporter, *an independent weekly journal that reports on the relationship between religion and society.*

In light of the September 11, 2001, terrorist attacks upon the United States and the subsequent outbursts from Muslim groups in response to Western aggression in the Middle East, most Americans consider Islamic radicals to be fundamentalists who have married religion to violence. In truth, Islamic fundamentalists enjoy popular support in Arab countries because of their reformist agendas and their opposition to Western-supported dictators. Fundamentalism thrives in the Middle East precisely because it counters Arab governments that have sacrificed Islamic values for secular benefits promoted by dealings with the United States and its allies. Islamist movements have also gained strength from their opposition to U.S. occupation of Arab lands and the many wars the West has supported in the Middle East. Until the United States recognizes that Islamic radicals have just grievances that can be best addressed by including Islamists in the political process, the volatile arm of political Islam will continue to attract large numbers of disgruntled adherents.

Margot Patterson, "Islamic Fundamentalism Feared, Misunderstood," *National Catholic Reporter*, October 8, 2004. Copyright © 2004 The National Catholic Reporter Publishing Company, 115 E. Armour Blvd., Kansas City, MO 64111. All rights reserved. Reproduced by permission of National Catholic Reporter, www.natcath.org.

Islamic fundamentalism has replaced communism as the enemy of the day. But despite the growing perception in this country that Islamic fundamentalism poses a threat to the United States, many Americans have only a minimal understanding of who Islamic fundamentalists are, what they believe and why their ranks continue to grow.

Misconceptions are common, with one-dimensional views of Islamic fundamentalists as violent extremists prevailing over more nuanced understandings of a movement that is complex and diverse.

In fact, most Islamic fundamentalists have much in common with their Christian counterparts, both perceiving reality through an interpretation of scripture that they view as inerrant. While some Islamic fundamentalists are recruited from the poor and uneducated, others come from middle class or prosperous backgrounds and have university degrees.

"The vast majority are not violent, bomb-throwing people. They are very much like your average very religious Catholic or Protestant," said Lawrence Davidson, professor of history at West Chester University in Pennsylvania and author of the book *Islamic Fundamentalism*.

"Islamist" movements . . . have developed increasing popular support as other efforts at economic and political reform in Muslim societies have failed.

Moving Beyond Religious Observance

For many Muslims, Islamic revival simply means becoming a more religiously observant Muslim. For others, being an observant Muslim is not simply more attention to prayer or fasting; it's also about creating a more just, moral, Islam-based society, said John Esposito, a professor of religion and international affairs at Georgetown University and founding director of the university's Center for Muslim-Christian Understanding.

Context, say scholars, is everything, and the political and economic climate that pertains in many Muslim countries, particularly in the Middle East, fuels Islamist movements that go beyond respect and reverence for the Islamic religion to adopt Islam as a political strategy or that refer to Islamic principles in calling for social and political reforms. These "Islamist" movements, as fundamentalism in the context of Islam is more properly called, have developed increasing popular support as other efforts at economic and political reform in Muslim societies have failed.

"If you held elections, in almost every single country in the Muslim world, Islamists would probably gain a majority. They would obtain a majority because they are highly organized, they have established an effective social base, and they are seen to be quite legitimate by a sizeable number of Muslims," said Fawaz Gerges, the Christian A. Johnson Chair in International Affairs and Middle Eastern Studies at Sarah Lawrence College and the author of the upcoming book *Jihadists: Unholy Warriors*. "The point to keep in mind is that Islamism is here to stay."

Scholars say Islamism represents for many Muslims a last-ditch effort to better their situation after decades of living in impoverished states that have experimented with socialism, Arab nationalism, military dictatorships and monarchies— with little discernible improvement in living standards for the vast majority of their populations.

"The socialists, the free marketers, the nationalists, the monarchists have failed," said Stephen Zunes, associate professor of politics at San Francisco University and author of *Tinderbox: U.S. Middle East Policy and the Roots of Terrorism.*

Islam appeals because it is an alternative to the secular nation-state, to a Western, non-indigenous, non-Islamic form of social organization and political process, said R. Scott Appleby, professor of history at the University of Notre Dame and co-editor of The Fundamentalism Project, a massive five-volume study of global fundamentalism.

It's one of the aftereffects of colonialism that the leaders of Muslim countries are often tied to Western political and economic interests as much as or more than to the people they govern.

How Fundamentalism Survives and Grows

But to become successful, Islamists face formidable obstacles, Appleby observed. He said most Muslims are wary of Islam as a political movement, oppose Islam's manipulation for violent or revolutionary ends, and don't have confidence in extreme Islamic movements.

"That means political Islam to be successful has a very narrow range of options," Appleby said. "On one hand, to mobilize large numbers of Muslims it must avoid revolutionary violence, which frightens and repulses Muslims who do not want Islam to be manipulated in that direction. On the other hand, political Muslims face virtually a police state that keeps them on a very short leash indeed and undermines or prohibits or cancels any kind of attempt to build a mass-based political party or movement."

Appleby said political Muslims are both feared and used by governments for their own ends. "For example, in the republics of the former Soviet Union like Tajikistan, Kyrgyzstan, Uzbekistan, these republics use anti-fundamentalism as a thin justification for incredible human rights abuses. Any person who is even moderately religious is labeled a fundamentalist, is imprisoned, hassled. It's been very difficult for many Muslim political parties to have any political effect."

Before 1967, Islamic fundamentalism was a relatively small movement. However, Israel's swift success over Egypt, Jordan and Syria in the Six Day War spelled the end of Arab nationalism as an effective political movement to which citizens throughout the Arab world could rally, while Israel's conquest of Jerusalem, the third-most holy site in Islam, transformed the Israeli-Palestinian conflict from a regional conflict into one that affected all Muslims. Other crises throughout the Muslim world—upheaval in Malaysia in 1969, Pakistan's invasion of Bangladesh in 1971, and later, the revolution in Iran and the Lebanese civil war—spurred the sense that the West had failed Muslim societies not only as an ally but as a viable model of development.

"There are those who say . . . it's one thing to borrow from the West; it's another thing to ape another people and culture and their either Christian or their secular values. So, religious revivalism grows and it's growing in societies that are overwhelmingly Muslim," said Esposito, who has written numerous books on Islam including *The Islamic Threat: Myth or Reality?*

"The slogan for many Islamists is Islam is the solution. In our own day, it's taken on a violent profile because Islam is being suppressed, quarantined, persecuted—most directly by the rulers of the nations where most Muslims live," said Appleby. "The history of Muslim-majority countries in the Mideast has been one of political leadership and governance that has increasingly been at odds, or seen to be at odds, with Islamic values."

[T]he United States must shift its focus from trying to crush radical Islamic movements militarily to pursing policies that discourage their development.

Casting off the Bonds of Colonialism

Indeed, it's one of the aftereffects of colonialism that the leaders of Muslim countries are often tied to Western political and economic interests as much as or more than to the people they govern.

Davidson noted that for a century or more most Muslims were ruled by colonial powers that managed their economies in such a way as to benefit themselves rather than the countries they ruled. When these Western states left, their place was taken by secular, Westernized elites they had developed who were often drawn from Christian business interests or from the ranks of the military.

"If you look at patterns of trade development in 17th, 18th and early 19th century in the Levant and in northern Egypt, the French and British preferred to work through middlemen who were often Christian—either Maronites, the Lebanese Catholics, or Coptic Christians in Egypt or Greek Orthodox. That doesn't mean all these elites as they grew up were Christian. There were also many Muslims who decided they would ally themselves with the powers that be. These were usually found from those seeking military careers."

Whatever the source, there grew up under colonial rule a Westernized elite whose leadership was culturally alienated from its own Muslim roots, Davidson said. "This was a very unsettling scenario for many religious Muslims, plus there was no economic improvement under either the colonial powers or the subsequent elites."

Davidson described the ruling elites as "businessmen who are concerned with making a profit and they don't feel a collective responsibility. Nobody has the big picture except the Islamic fundamentalists. They have populist roots.

"A lot of these organizations started as community-based self-help projects. If you look at the Muslim Brotherhood [of Egypt], what did they do? Even today, it runs medical clinics, job training programs, subsidizes cheap food, collects garbage. It does things the government doesn't. Religious groups are very popular because they are meeting the needs. They go into politics. They meet violent resistance, and they react violently," said Davidson.

Reacting against Oppressive Regimes

Algeria is a case in point. There, Islamists formed a political party, but once they succeeded in democratic elections, the election was abrogated and the party outlawed. Violence ensued, and a bloody civil war began.

"The elites don't want to lose their privileged position. They are also afraid of the lifestyle changes that would certainly be brought about if fundamentalists come to power. The women are afraid of that especially," Davidson said.

Ironically, while radical Islamic groups have recently come to the forefront of policy concerns in Washington, the United States has frequently encouraged such movements either by outright support, as in Afghanistan where the U.S.-supported mujahideen efforts to oust the Soviet Union, or by supporting oppressive regimes that then trigger a backlash both against the government and against the United States for supporting it, as in Iran.

Today, said Gerges, the main beneficiaries of the U.S. invasion and occupation of Iraq are not moderates or secularists but Islamists calling for resistance and jihad against the U.S. occupiers and their supporters. "Iraqi society is being Islamicized from within because of the American invasion and occupation of Iraq," said Gerges.

Zunes said that extremist Islam arises out of either of two conditions.

"One is political repression. Countries where Islamic parties have been allowed to compete in elections, in Jordan or Yemen or some of the South Asian countries, they've tended to be fairly moderate and responsible in terms of parliamentary debate. When they're forced underground and suppressed, in Uzbekistan, Saudi Arabia, that's where they get violent and extreme. The second variable is in areas where there's been mass dislocation—Afghanistan, Lebanon, Palestine—or screwed-up economic policies. Economic dislocation feeds fundamentalism. The social message of the Quran is a lot easier to understand than Marxist dialectics."

A Shift in U.S. Policies Is Needed

Like Gerges, Zunes notes extremist forces have also arisen because of wars that the United States has supported. Hezbollah in Lebanon and Hamas in Palestine are two examples he cites. Radical Islam was not a force in Lebanon before the Israeli invasion of 1982; Hamas similarly owes its emergence and influence to the ongoing Israeli occupation of the Palestinian territories.

In an article titled "U.S. Policy Toward Political Islam" in the journal *Foreign Policy in Focus*, Zunes argues that the United States must shift its focus from trying to crush radical Islamic movements militarily to pursing policies that discourage their development.

[M]any American policymakers are unwilling to support the kind of changes that would enable Islamists to come to power.

"The U.S. must clearly understand the reasons why a small but dangerous minority of Muslims have embraced extremist ideologies and violent tactics. These movements are often rooted in legitimate grievances voiced by underrepresented and oppressed segments of the population, particularly the poor. And the U.S. is increasingly identified with the political, social and economic forces that are responsible for their misery," Zunes wrote.

Other scholars concur that U.S. policy is aggravating rather than minimizing conflict with Islamic extremism. The war with Iraq, support for Israel, and the U.S. military presence in the Gulf—perceived as neocolonialism—feeds anti-Americanism among Muslims while the negative stereotypes of Islam that have developed in the United States since 9/11 have led to a state of mutual fear and suspicion between Americans and Muslims.

University of Chicago historian Martin Marty, co-editor of The Fundamentalism Project, notes that the hard-line rhetoric adopted by the [George W.] Bush administration—references to the "axis of evil" and "you're either with us or against us"—aggravates divisions between the Muslim world and the West and glosses over the real frictions that exist within the Islamic world itself. At the same time, continuing U.S. support for Israel's occupation of the West Bank and Gaza Strip confirms many Muslims' belief that the United States is hostile to their interests and hypocritical in its support for democracy.

"American policy toward Israel fuels Islamist sentiment. As long as we're uncritical, as long as we side with them, as long as we let the peace process die, it shows that we're out to do the Palestinians in," said Marty.

While the Bush administration says it has embraced democratization in the Middle East as a goal, it remains an open question whether Islamists will be allowed to take their place at the political table. Like many of the authoritarian rulers in the Middle East that the United States is allied with, many American policymakers are unwilling to support the kind of changes that would enable Islamists to come to power. Repression then fuels extremism, some scholars say.

The corrective to militant Islamism is to integrate mainstream Islamists into the political process of their respective countries, Gerges said.

"If you include mainstream Islamists, you present a peaceful alternative to the jihadist current," Gerges said. "You cannot have a healthy political process in the Middle East without these mainstream Islamists playing a part because they present some of the most powerful voices in the political life of their countries."

For now, most countries in the Arab and Muslim world continue to exclude even moderate Islamists from power. "These dictatorial regimes are still very much in control of forces of coercion—military, police. As long as they can manage to do that, they can decimate the ranks of Islamist leaders. But in the long run, it's hard to predict," Davidson said. "Islamic fundamentalism as a belief is growing."

5

Muslims Should Reject Islamism

Amil Imani

Amil Imani is an Iranian-born, pro-democracy activist who re-sides in the United States. He is a poet, writer, literary transla-tor, novelist, and essayist who has been writing and speaking out for the struggling people of his native land.

Muslims have had their faith forced-fed to them by religious leaders with violent and oppressive motives. This has kept most of the Islamic world in a state of slavery, leaving Muslims with-out the freedom to choose how to worship or how to pursue their own lives. While most of the faithful are not devoted to the radi-cal causes of their leaders, their silence and their fear of asserting independence props up fundamentalist regimes. It is time for Muslims to join the free people of the world to defeat radical Is-lam.

Dear Muslims, your right to think for yourself and choose what you believe was denied to you from birth. In re-turn, your mind was crammed, without let up, with constant threats of dreadful punishments if you tried to retrieve your rights and promises of glorious rewards if you meekly ac-cepted the collaborative action of your parents, relatives, and the vested-interest clergy.

You became a Muslim, by accident of birth, although above all else you are a human being. You have the right and the ob-ligation to examine the belief implanted in you and to decide for yourself if it is the guidance you want.

Amil Imani, "A Call to Moderate Muslims," *Islam Watch*, April 8, 2007. Reproduced by permission.

This is the 21st century. The vast planet earth of the time of Muhammad has shrunk into a global village. The greatly diverse and disparate peoples of the world are now neighbors in the same village. This new tribe of the global village is facing immense challenges and opportunities. The resources and the talents of the various clans can no longer be squandered on internecine fighting. Every member of every clan, irrespective of gender, race, or any other consideration is entitled to full citizenship, a just citizenship that bestows privileges and demands responsibilities.

Islamism Is a Sinister Form of Slavery

Radical Islam claims to be the true Islam and strives to force humanity into submission to a system of beliefs and practices of Sharia which are anathema to freedom. Even Muslims who do not agree with the extremist Islam are intimidated, pressured into silence, and condemned to death.

Hardly a week passes without a Grand Mufti or an Ayatollah issuing pronouncements in support of radical Islam.

"The world is a dangerous place not because of those who do evil, but because of those who look on and do nothing," said Albert Einstein. It is incumbent on every Muslim to arise and counter Islamism. In this courageous effort, the non-Islamist Muslims can count on the unflagging support of free people.

The problem facing humanity today is reminiscent of an earlier and equally sinister practice of slavery in America. A handful of northern whites, motivated by the high human ideals of freedom and justice, rose against slavery. They were the abolitionists who believed that slavery was evil. The abolitionists risked a great deal fighting to free the terribly-wronged black people. Over time, the movement gathered momentum, more and more black people shattered the shackles of slavery and banded with more and more awakened non-slaves to put an end to the horrific scourge of slavery.

Free people are committed to defend the rights of Muslims to observe peaceful Islam because they believe in the sanctity of freedom. By standing for Muslims' legitimate human rights, free people also guard their own freedom.

Today's scourge is the radical Islam that denies the non-Muslims as well as the moderate Muslims the inalienable right of freedom, freedom to choose whom and how to worship, how to live in harmony with people who make different choices, and how to pool together in overcoming the myriad of challenges that demand humanity's united and best efforts.

The word "jihad" has at least two vastly different meanings. It means exertion. It also stands for making war, and it is the latter that the jihadists invoke as their mandate.

Preaching Fear and Violence

While the moderate Muslims are generally silent, either out of fear, lack of organization, or apathy, the Islamists work around the clock and around the world to further their agenda. Hardly a week passes without a Grand Mufti or an Ayatollah issuing pronouncements in support of radical Islam. The rank-and-file Islamist clergy, for their part, transmit these fatwas and edicts to their flocks in mosques and hammer them into the minds of impressionable children in madressehs [Islamic schools]. Through this grass-root process, radical Islam is recruiting greater and greater numbers of adherents. On the one hand, the Islamists engage in acts of violence to disrupt the functioning of societies, while on the other they cleverly exploit the freedom they enjoy in non-Islamic lands to subvert them from within.

As a moderate Muslim, you can no longer remain a spectator in the existential clash of Islamism with freedom. The best guarantee for you to practice Islam as a religion of peace is to rally with those who are guardians of freedom. You also need to examine what kind of life the Islamists aim to impose, by whatever means they can, on everyone. Even a partial brief examination of what constitutes radical Islam should be enough to persuade every righteous Muslim to oppose and defeat it.

The great majority of Muslims are not adherents of the radical line. Yet because the Islamists wage their war under the name of Islam, they receive immense direct and indirect support from the rank-and-file ordinary Muslims. It is this support of moderate Muslims that keeps the Islamists alive. And it is the Islamists who intend to show no mercy to any and all who do not share their theology, be they Muslims or not.

The brand of Islam that the Islamists hold sacred, whether of the numerous Sunni or many Shia varieties, is replete with beliefs and practices that range from the absurd to the profane. It is a great travesty to any human to be forced to adopt the entire package of the Islamists' dictates.

The Islamists have searched the scripture and have selectively chosen those statements and precedence that they could use to legitimize their violent and primitive agenda. The Jihadists, for instance, claim that the Quran itself urges them to make jihad, "jahedoo fee sabeil-u-llah," make jihad for the cause of Allah. The word "jihad" has at least two vastly different meanings. It means exertion. It also stands for making war, and it is the latter that the jihadists invoke as their mandate.

Absurd and Dangerous Pronouncements

The Sunni radicalism is directed by a host of movements such as Wahabism, Al Qaeda, Hamas, and the Moslem Brotherhood. For now, however, let us take a brief-look at Shia radicalism based on the teachings and pronouncements of the late Ayatollah Khomeini of Iran, a man revered by the world's Shia as "Imam," a title that has been exclusive to the twelve successive descendants of Muhammad who headed the sect. Shia theologians as well as the rank-and-file faithful view Khomeini's writings and sayings as religiously authoritative, illuminating, and binding. It is instructive to list a few teachings of this most-revered and exalted cleric who has been the father of Shia radicalism and a point-man in the war against all people he deemed as infidels.

"Islam alone is to govern."

"We must give rise to repeated crises, and give a new and better value to the idea of death and martyrdom. . . . If Iran disappears in the future, it is not important; what is important is to drown the whole world in a situation of crisis."

"Those who want to set up democracy want to drag our country into corruption and perdition. They are worse than the Jews. They must be hanged. They are not men. They have the blood of animals. Be they damned."

"All the laws in the world, except those of the Islamic republic, come from a handful of idiotic syphilitics. They are null and void. Islam does not recognize any other law but its own in the world."

This man of great adulation and emulation of the Islamists, Khomeini, was indeed a bloodthirsty as well as an ignorant person who issued great many dangerous and absurd pronouncements that are taken as edicts and laws to be followed by the faithful. Some examples are:

He gave order to the Iranian Air Force to destroy American satellites, and ordered the ministry of agriculture to flood the American market with Iranian wheat so as to make the economy of the "Great Satan" dependent on (Iranian wheat), even though Iran itself has usually been importer of wheat.

A great deal of Khomeini's adjudications are concerned with matters such as the way to urinate and to defecate; what is pure and what is impure; women and their periods; sexuality with animals.

The hatred of Khomeini for the Jews surpassed that of Hitler. He proclaimed:

"Israel must burn to ashes."

Armageddon Agenda

It is from this command that his devoted pupil, the fascist [Iranian] president [Mahmoud] Ahmadinejad, gets his marching orders to "wipe Israel off the map." Before Ahmadinejad, another president of the Islamic Republic of Iran, mullah Ali Akbar Refsanjani, announced that a nuclear exchange will destroy Israel while the Islamic world can tolerate and survive the damage.

This sort of Armageddon-thinking and agenda is not exclusive to the Shia Islamists. The Sunni jihadists' program is just as regressive, oppressive, and violent.

In conclusion, dear moderate Muslim, if this is not your Islam, if you do not subscribe to its tenets and plans, and you do not want to live under the barbaric provisions of Sharia, then you need to speak up, rise up, and actively confront it. You can be assured that the free people of the world are committed to join rank with you to defeat radical Islam.

6

The United States Must Defeat Islamism

Edward Cline

A U.S. Air Force veteran, Edward Cline is a novelist best known for his Sparrowhawk series of novels set in England and Virginia during the Revolutionary War period.

Islamists comprise a cunning force that carries out a murderous ideology both in the Arab world and within the free-societies of the West. To effectively counter the threat of Islamic terrorism, the United States and its allies cannot be content with hunting down small cells of radicals. Instead, the West should strike at the heart of Islam, toppling those Arab regimes that support or simply tolerate Islamism. If the capitals of Islamist indoctrination can be shut down, the individual activists will lack funding and guidance and eventually dissipate.

In *Toilers of the Sea*, one of Victor Hugo's lesser-known novels, is a marvelous description of how to defeat an enemy that is insidious by its nature, an enemy that has served as a symbol of the banal parasitism of evil. Towards the end of the novel, Gilliatt, the hero, is seized in an underwater cave by a devilfish, or octopus. The creature's tentacles cling to Gilliatt, and it is about to pierce his chest with its beak:

> "The devilfish is cunning. It first tries to stupefy its prey. It seizes, then waits as long as it can.

> Gilliatt held his knife. The suction increased.

Edward Cline, "The Devilfish of Islamofascism," *Capitalism*, August 16, 2005. Capitalism Magazine. Reproduced by permission. www.capmag.com.

All at once the creature detached its sixth tentacle from the rock, launched it at him, and attempted to seize his left arm. . . . At the same time, it thrust its head forward swiftly. . . .

But Gilliatt was on his guard. Being watched, he watched.

Gilliatt plunged the point of his knife into the flat, viscous mass, and with a twisting movement similar to the flourish of a whip, describing a circle around the two eyes, he tore out the head as one wrenches out a tooth.

It was finished. The whole creature dropped. . . . The four hundred suckers simultaneously released their hold of the rock and the man.

This rag sank to the bottom."

Islam Is Not a Peaceful Religion

It is a passage our leaders ought to be made to read and learn from if they wish to successfully prosecute the "war against terrorism." The advocates and promulgators of Islamofascism, like the devilfish, stupefy their prey, and wait, then strike. Missing from the real life dilemma is a Gilliatt. President [George W.] Bush is not one, nor is Prime Minister Tony Blair of Britain. They attack the tentacles but, in the name of tolerance, refuse to cut off the head.

It would be interesting to know how many American Muslims are willing to don [bomb-laden] rucksacks and commit . . . sabotage here.

As many contributors to [*Capitalism Magazine*] have pointed out, most recently and succinctly by Dr. Edwin Locke and Alex Epstein in their penetrating "The Terrorists' Motivation: Islam," the trouble is not that killers have "hijacked a peaceful religion." The trouble is that Islam is not, in its fundamental tenets (if its virulent injunctions can be called "principles"), a "peaceful" religion. It is a manifesto for the conquest and destruction of all Western civilization and the establishment of a global anti-man, anti-mind theocracy.

It pursues this goal, it should be apparent by now, by employing two methods: with immediate, violent action, such as indiscriminate bombings; and by an osmotic process of invading a Western country with a fifth column that works to alter Western laws to tolerate its presence, while at the same time preaching the abandonment of those laws in favor of law based on an intolerant Koran.

The Koran cannot be compromised, repudiated piecemeal, or "modified" so that it posed no threat to the West. It cannot be "secularized" without destroying Islam. Islam can no more be "perverted" or "hijacked" than can Nazism, Fascism, or Japanese Bushido. Islamic clerics know this, as well as rank-and-file Muslims, which is why they are largely silent on the matter of terrorism, with the exception of an occasional equivocating expression of public regret for the bombings.

Attack Militant Islam at Its Source

The most serious problem is that the current conflict is being treated as a mere "war against terrorism." It has devolved into a mere cops-and-robbers manhunt for terrorists and suspected terrorists and their cells. It may as well be put on a par with a campaign to stamp out "violent bank robberies."

This is not to deprecate the heroic efforts of Britain's authorities in tracking down the London "Islamikazies" of 7/7 [who planted bombs on London subways in July 2005], which includes a "shoot to kill" standing order and the suspension of "racial profiling" to identify suspects. But that is merely rounding up and obstructing the "foot soldiers" of the Islamafascists. The parties guilty of associating with the 7/7 bombers, and with the ones who botched a second round of London bombings and who are on the run, can be replaced, according to a British report, from among 16,000 militant British Muslims.

It would be interesting to know how many American Muslims are willing to don rucksacks and commit the same sabotage here. It is possible that such a report has been written and circulated among those agencies charged with identifying and "neutralizing" such "activists." But, for fear of offending American Muslims, very likely President Bush has forbidden its publication.

After Saddam Hussein and his government had been overthrown, we should have moved on to Syria or Iran and let the Iraqis sort out what to do next.

If we are at war with an insidious ideology, why limit our self-preservation actions to policing an invading army, while neglecting the goals and ends of its leaders?

The octopus head of Islamofascism is: Iran, Syria, and Saudi Arabia. To a lesser extent, one must include Pakistan and even Afghanistan, since the Taliban are apparently still active in both those countries and the heads of those countries are impotent or unwilling to eradicate them.

Most of the madrasses [Islamic schools] in Pakistan are subsidized by Saudi Arabia, are a chief source of suicide bombers. One might argue that Iraq was a good starting place to eradicate our enemy. But why the U.S. should be expending lives and fortune to establish a "democratic" government there, beggars explanation and reason. After Saddam Hussein and his government had been overthrown [in Iraq], we should have moved on to Syria or Iran and let the Iraqis sort out what to do next. We are under no moral obligation to help anyone discover the benefits of Western institutions, not at the price of sacrificing American lives, American wealth, and American liberties, which is what is occurring now.

Our leaders must recognize that the head must be lopped off before any substantive progress can be made against alien or resident terrorists. Until they learn that lesson, the bombings and killings and mayhem will continue unabated. The devilfish has watched, waited, and struck repeatedly ever since the World Trade Center bombing of 1993. It has taken the measure of our resolve and of our ignorance. It is neither shocked nor awed.

If the Source of Islam Is Destroyed, Its Radicals Will Dissipate

Now, a very strange thing happened when Admiral Karl Donitz arranged the German surrender to the Allies in 1945; the European war was over.

Another strange thing happened when General Douglas MacArthur received the Japanese surrender on the battleship Missouri in 1945; the Pacific war was ended.

And a third strange thing occurred when World War Two was declared over and became history; the Allies ceased worrying that the war would continue within the borders of their own countries.

The heads were lopped off, the tentacles died when the primitive brain that guided them was gone, and the rags of Nazism and Bushido sank to the bottom.

Whatever fifth columnists and sympathizers existed in the U.S. and Britain did not carry on the fight for Nazism or the Emperor after German and Japanese governments had surrendered and were reconstituted. Many Nazis fled justice to South America, to Egypt, and other safe havens. And the Allies did not wring their hands over "human rights" and trials until after the war, in Nuremberg. Then it was the rights of the millions of murdered that concerned the judges, not the rights of the accused members of the governments guilty of those crimes.

The same thing would happen to Islam, if the West had enough self-esteem and resolve to fight the war as it should be fought: by taking the war to the enemy. Islam would scurry back into its self-made Dark Age and pose no threat to those who wished to live without vengeful mullahs and imams looking over their shoulders. Muslims who chose to remain in the West would need to learn to submit to Western laws of individual rights and the separation of church and state. If they do not choose to submit to those laws, they should be invited to emigrate to those nations whose ethics and society are more fitting to their refusal to think.

Whatever Islamic terrorist cells might exist in the U.S., Britain, France and other Western nations, would wither away for lack of funding, guidance and even purpose. They would not and could not "carry on the fight."

The West Must Be Vigilant and Determined

Where would the West be today if Churchill and Roosevelt were stupefied and adopted the Bush/Blair philosophy of fighting an enemy intent on conquest? Where would we be if they had restricted their combat operations to fighting saboteurs, provocateurs and secret agents on the "home front"? Where would we be if they had not judged Nazism and Bushido as inimical to Western civilization?

Would we have won World War Two if we had "tolerated" Nazism and Japanese imperialism as multiculturalist "peers" of our own political system, and merely sought to prevent their saboteurs from bombing schools and subways? Would we have won if we regarded Nazism as just another "belief system" that was "hijacked" by Hitler?

Where would the West be today if Churchill and Roosevelt had adopted the Bush/Blair method of confronting our enemies?

I am certain of this: I would not be asking these questions. I might not be. I might have been liquidated for refusing to bow to the Emperor or to shout "Sieg heil!"

And I have ample proof of my possible fate should I refuse to bow to Mecca. That is why I will not discard my knife of reason and my love of existence.

7

The United States Must Not Appease Islamism

David Kupelian

David Kupelian is vice president and managing editor of World-NetDaily *Web site and* Whistleblower *magazine, two independent news organizations. He is also the author of* The Marketing of Evil: How Radicals, Elitists, and Pseudo-Experts Sell Us Corruption Disguised as Freedom.

In the war against radical Islam, the United States and its allies need to be confident that the conflict is justified. Islamism threatens the world, and this threat must be eliminated; however, many people in the United States are losing faith in the rightness of this cause and are not willing to accept the sacrifices required to defeat the enemy. Some have come to the conclusion that the Islamists are the true victims of Western aggression; others are simply worn down from the years of bloodshed. Yet there can be no appeasement with terrorists, for to do so would show weakness and embolden the Islamists to stage more violent acts to get more concessions from Western leaders. The United States must show its strength by standing up to the Islamists and demonstrate a concerted will to force radical Islam into submission.

I'm looking at a photograph of a beautiful young Christian girl who has just been beheaded by a gang of six rampaging, machete-wielding Muslim radicals.

Her bloody body is lying on an autopsy table. A few inches to the left of her torso lies her severed head, nestled in a

David Kupelian, "The Real Secret to Defeating Radical Islam," *WorldNetDaily*, November 21, 2005. Reproduced by permission. www.wnd.com.

bunched-up black plastic trash bag. Delicate features, lovely dark hair matted with blood, eyes closed, her face appears sad and almost serene, prompting one to reflect on the incomprehensible brutality and terror she must have experienced.

Two other teenage girls, both Christian, were also decapitated during the same Oct. 29 [2005] massacre on the Indonesian island of Sulawesi. The Muslim men, all dressed in black, savagely attacked the 16- to 19-year-old girls with machetes as they walked across a cocoa plantation on their way to the private Christian school they attended. Their heads were found some distance from the bodies, the head of one girl discarded mockingly in front of a Christian church.

Islamic attacks on Christians, including May's bombing in the nearby, predominantly Christian town of Tentena that killed 22 and injured over 30, are common in this area—with over 40 local attacks in the last two-and-a-half years. Analysts say Muslim militants are targeting central Sulawesi because they see it as a likely foundation for an Islamic state.

Global Jihad

This scene, with all its attendant horror, is being duplicated *all over the world*, from Israel to India, from Russia to the Philippines, from Sudan to the Balkans, and right on into the heart of Europe with massive Muslim rioting in France [in 2005] and the terrorist train bombing in Spain [in 2004], plus the subway bombings in London [in 2005]—and of course the 9-11 attacks in America that killed 3,000 [in 2001]. Violent Islamic jihad, dormant for centuries, is once again on the move worldwide.

Islam has attempted global domination before. In past centuries it conquered not only Arabia, Persia, Syria and Egypt, but major parts of Africa, Asia and Europe, until it was ultimately defeated and lost its will to conquer—for a time, anyway.

And it's not just during Muhammad's era, or later medieval times, that militant Islam has savagely attacked neighboring cultures, either butchering "infidels" (non-Muslims) outright or converting them at the point of the sword. Jihad has always been a part of Islam.

For Americans, largely ignorant of world history, Islamic radicalism mysteriously appeared on their television screens for the first time on Sept. 11, 2001, and has dominated our national security concerns ever since. But for those more familiar with the major forces shaping world events, the violent spread of Islam is recognized as one of the most important geopolitical forces in the last 14 centuries, one that has touched billions of lives.

For instance, I personally lost dozens of family members—perhaps over 100—in the genocide of the Christian Armenians by the Muslim Turks. I'll mention just one of those family members—my great grandfather, Steelianos Leondiades. A Protestant minister, in 1908 he was attending a conference of Armenian and Greek ministers in the major Turkish city of Adana. Here's how his daughter, my maternal grandmother Anna Paulson, recalled the terrible events that unfolded: "Some of the Turkish officers came to the conference room and told all these ministers—there were 70 of them, ministers and laymen and a few wives: 'If you embrace the Islamic religion you will all be saved. If you don't, you will all be killed.'"

Steelianos, my great grandfather, acting as a spokesman for the ministers group asked the Turks for 15 minutes so they could make their decision. During that time the ministers and their companions talked, read the Bible to each other and prayed. In the end, none of them would renounce their Christian faith and convert to Islam.

"And then," Anna recalled, "they were all killed.

"They were not even buried. They were all thrown down the ravine."

The only way we know any details of this massacre—one of many during that hellish period when 1.5 million Armenians were exterminated—is because one victim survived the ordeal. "One man woke up, he wasn't dead," my grandmother said. "He woke up and got up and said, 'Brethren, brethren, is there anybody alive here? I'm alive, come on, let's go out together.'" Had it not been for that survivor's account, no one would have known the circumstances of this modern-day martyrdom.

(By the way, details of the appalling decapitations of the three Christian girls in Indonesia also emerged thanks to a lone survivor—a fourth student who was also attacked and severely injured, but who survived to tell authorities about the attack.)

My great grandfather was a martyr, a real one. But today, we most often hear the word "martyr" being used to describe hypnotized Islamic jihadis who commit unspeakable mass atrocities against innocent people while dementedly chanting "*Allahu Akhbar, Allahu Akhbar, Allahu Akhbar*" to drown out what's left of their conscience.

That's not martyrdom. It's terrorism—and it's about time we realized what terrorism is all about.

There's a funny thing about appeasement. It's hard to give in to evil without first agreeing with that evil, at least a little.

How Terrorism Works

On one level, terrorism works by simply causing us so much pain, suffering and dread of future terror that we eventually weaken and give in to the terrorists' demands. But the ultimate goal of terrorism is to capture our hearts and minds—to convert us.

What? How can terrorizing us transform our attitudes in *favor* of the terrorists' viewpoint? Wouldn't we recoil in horror and, if anything, move farther away from sympathy toward the perpetrators? Not necessarily.

Remember, militant Muslims "convert" individuals to Islam by threat of death. Why shouldn't they try the same tactic on entire societies?

Stop and consider what happens when we're intimidated and frightened by terrorism, or even the threat of it. Wonder of wonders, some of us start to sympathize with our enemy.

There's a funny thing about appeasement. It's hard to give in to evil without first agreeing with that evil, at least a little. We have to allow our minds to be bent, our previous values and perceptions altered, even slightly; we somehow have to see the terrorists as not quite totally evil. "*Yes, they may be angry and even murderous, but after all, don't they have legitimate grievances against us? Maybe we brought on this attack by our past actions. Maybe we're at fault. Maybe their cause is just. Maybe we're the real terrorists.*"

Does that sound like an exaggeration? Do you remember Cindy Sheehan, so lionized by America's "mainstream press" as the courageous public face of the antiwar movement? She referred to Islamic terrorists flocking to Iraq to kill American soldiers as "freedom fighters." Meanwhile she calls the president of the United States a "lying bastard," a "jerk," an "evil maniac," a "gangster," a "war criminal," a "murderous thug" and—of course—a "terrorist."

To become an appeaser, you have to sympathize with the enemy, either overtly like Sheehan, or secretly. How else can you look at yourself in the mirror and justify giving in to evil?

The question is, how do we come to side with those who are intent on destroying us?

Sympathizing with the Enemy

On Aug. 23, 1973, a submachine-gun-toting escaped convict named Jan-Erik Olsson attempted to rob a bank in Stockholm, Sweden, and in the process took four hostages.

Incredibly, over the course of their five-and-a-half day captivity, the hostages developed a strong bond with Olsson and another ex-con who joined him—so much so that they came to sympathize with and support the criminals holding them captive at gunpoint, while fearing and disparaging the police who sought to free them. Some of the captives later testified on behalf of, or raised money for, the legal defense of their captors.

Could it be that many people are so intimidated by radical Islam . . . that their fear is transformed unconsciously into a strange sympathy and support for the terrorists . . .?

This phenomenon of captives developing an emotional bond with their captors, dubbed the "Stockholm Syndrome" after the bank hostage case, has been observed in many hostage situations over the years, and has also shed light on other seemingly inexplicable behaviors, such as battered wives who identify with and defend horribly abusive husbands.

Characteristics of the Stockholm Syndrome include:

1. The captives start to identify with their captors, at first as a means of survival, calculating that the captor won't hurt them if they are cooperative and supportive.

2. The captives realize a rescue attempt is dangerous and could result in their being hurt or even killed, and so they come to fear and oppose efforts to rescue them.

3. Longer-term captivity fosters an emotional attachment to the captor, as the victims learn of the captor's problems and grievances, as well as his hopes and aspirations. In some cases, the captives come to identify with and believe in the justness of the captor's "cause."

Is it possible that the Stockholm Syndrome—where victims are so intimidated and fearful that they end up sympathizing with and defending those threatening their lives, and disparaging those brave souls trying to save them—might help explain some of what has happened worldwide in response to the murderous outrages of radical Islam?

Could it be that many people are so intimidated by radical Islam, so fearful of being victims themselves, that their fear is transformed unconsciously into a strange sympathy and support for the terrorists, in an attempt to placate them?

If you cower before a bully in an attempt to placate him, all you accomplish is to make him more confident, more demanding, more contemptuous of you. . . .

Could this be a factor in the absurd political correctness we see in America and Europe with regard to Islam?

- Why is it that since 9-11, increasing numbers of students on American college campuses are extolling the "Palestinian cause" and condemning Israel as a terrorist state, with some schools even hosting thinly disguised jihad recruitment rallies by radical Islamic groups?

- Why is it that Muslims can riot day after day in and around Paris, burn over a thousand cars, ransack businesses and schools, rampage through 300 towns shooting at police and firemen—and the international press barely mentions that the rioters are Muslims?

- Why is it that every time a terror incident occurs in the U.S.—such as the Beltway snipers that terrorized the Washington, D.C., metropolitan area for weeks [in 2002]—the government and press bend over backwards to downplay any possible Islamic jihad connection? (The key Beltway sniper had converted to Islam, changed his name to "Muhammad" and had known sympathies for Islamic terrorists.)

- Why do the government and news media treat the Council for American-Islamic Relations, CAIR, as a legitimate civil rights organization when it has been identified by two former FBI counterterrorism chiefs as a "front group" for Hamas [a Palestinian organization calling for the destruction of Israel], and several of its leaders have been convicted on federal terrorism charges since 9-11?

If you consider Americans' understandable fear of radical Muslims, and add to that fear our culture's knee-jerk multicultural dread of being perceived as "racist," you can start to understand today's bizarre deference to Islam in the West.

Losing the Will to Fight

Somehow, the West has lost its courage and has been intimidated by radical Islam into trying to appease it. It's easy for this to happen—even in a battle-hardened nation like Israel.

Once the Jewish state set the standard for the entire world in how to deal with terrorism. But in recent years Israel's leadership, along with a considerable segment of public opinion, have been seduced into pursuing appeasement as the road to peace.

Appeasement always encourages *violence.*

Understandably, Israelis are tired and worn down after more than 50 years of fighting and dying just to defend their right to exist. But the problem is, the more Israel tries to display good will and make concessions for peace with the surrounding Arab states, the more terrorist attacks on Israeli civilians *increase.* Shouldn't the opposite occur? Wouldn't you think the more land giveaways and other concessions the Israelis make, the closer they would get to peace? No, the result is more terror and more pressure for more concessions.

Look at this simple and familiar syndrome on a personal level: If you cower before a bully in an attempt to placate him, all you accomplish is to make him more confident, more demanding, more contemptuous of you—in other words, your weakness literally transforms him into an even bigger and more dangerous bully.

Israel has made a string of major concessions—the most recent being the unprecedented, unilateral gift of Gaza to the Palestinians [in 2005]. Are the Palestinians happy as a result? Are they grateful to Israel? No, Gaza is becoming a Mecca for terrorists, a prime Middle East staging area for ever more terror attacks. Hamas and other terror groups believe they are seeing the fruits of their murderous attacks on Israelis—and are encouraged now to engage in more terrorism until they have "liberated" all of Israel, which they call "Palestine."

Appeasement always *encourages* violence. If more violence is not immediately forthcoming in response to appeasement, it's only a strategic delay. Israel should have learned this lesson from hard experience, such as when it made its disastrous, unilateral withdrawal from southern Lebanon, which resulted in widespread death among Lebanese Christians and the emboldening of the Hezbollah terror army.

The simple fact is, just as with Communists and Nazis, Islamo-fascists regard goodwill gestures and concessions as nothing more than contemptible weakness and an irresistible invitation to take advantage. Hitler, shortly after the appeasing [British Prime Minister Neville] Chamberlain arrived home proudly displaying his worthless peace treaty, turned around and attacked Britain. In the same way, Islamic militants consider it just good strategy to lie and break treaties.

It seems somewhere along the line [Israeli Prime Minister] Ariel Sharon forgot what he wrote in his autobiography, "Warrior." Reflecting on his years as a daring soldier fighting for his nation's survival, Sharon wrote that, in dealing with Israel's Arab attackers, he "came to view the objective not simply as retaliation, or even deterrence in the usual sense. It was to create in the Arabs a psychology of defeat, to beat them every time and to beat them so decisively that they would develop the conviction they could never win."

Now we're getting somewhere.

Terrorism is intimidation. The terrorists' end-game is to so frighten us that we not only cower in fear, but are *converted*—that is, our fear actually causes a change in our attitudes and beliefs regarding the terrorists and their cause.

Forcing the Enemy to Submit

The antidote to this intimidation factor is self-evident: Terrorists (intimidators) must be super-intimidated into submission. Sorry, but it's the only language they speak. Anything else besides overwhelming, paralyzing, courage-destroying strength is perceived by them as weakness.

[T]he biggest danger to this nation in the global war against radical Islam is the specter of appeasement—in all its forms.

For example: In 1986, after America had suffered many casualties from a long string of terror activities fomented by Libyan leader Muammar al-Qaddafi, President Reagan bombed Libya. Called Operation El Dorado Canyon, the U.S. raids targeted specific sites, including Qaddafi's house, and killed 60 people, including Qaddafi's adopted four-year-old daughter.

As a result, most historians agree, Libya basically abandoned terrorism, with the notable exception of the bombing of Pan Am Flight 103 over Lockerbie, Scotland [in 1988], for which Libya formally accepted responsibility in 2003, paying each victim's family $8 million.

OK, you might well say, we can agree you have to crush terrorism so badly it can't get up. But what about efforts to influence the hearts and minds of the larger Muslim world—to nudge them toward moderation and away from radicalism and violence? Of course, such efforts are essential to prevailing long-term in the current clash of civilizations, a war that rages not just between Islam and the West, but between radical Islam and that religion's more moderate, modern elements. The great majority of Muslims worldwide, even those somewhat sympathetic to militant Islam, might well be susceptible to moving toward a more moderate worldview.

But whatever educational outreach the West might employ to the Muslim world to champion the joys of freedom and self-determination, of tolerance and women's rights and so on—and for that matter, whatever outreach moderate Muslims make to their Islamic brothers and sisters—they're all useless without the accompanying demoralization and destruction of the violent jihad movement.

Let's learn a lesson from America's "Greatest Generation."

One of the most controversial actions in U.S. military history was dropping the atomic bomb on Hiroshima and Nagasaki to break the will of the maniacal Japanese war effort. Now, I know there are persuasive arguments both for and against America having used the atomic bomb in this way. But whether or not you agree, in retrospect, with the bombings of those two Japanese cities, what is undeniable is that doing so accomplished more than end the war with Japan. It broke Japan. It confronted the "evil spirit" that had possessed that nation—with its crazed kamikaze suicide pilots and its emperor who was regarded as a god—and it violently exorcized it. Having neutralized the evil that had captivated Japan, America became that nation's friend and helped massively reconstruct it, ultimately turning Japan into the civilized, successful, First World economic power it is today.

For that matter, after the Allies annihilated Hitler's war machine and along with it the German will and capacity to attack its neighbors, the U.S. also helped a newly sober Germany to become a great Western power. Our enemies, Japan and Germany, became our friends.

Once again, I am not saying "Nuke Mecca" or anything of the sort. I am saying what Ariel Sharon said years ago: We must create in the enemy "a psychology of defeat, to beat them every time and to beat them so decisively that they would develop the conviction they could never win."

No More Vietnams

Of course, I am not preaching this sermon to America's military, which knows the truth of what I am saying here far better than I do. But, to America's citizens and political leadership, I'm saying the biggest danger to this nation in the global war against radical Islam is the specter of appeasement—in all its forms.

[The] global jihad can succeed only if we lose the battle for hearts and minds—our own.

Remember, winning any war is not just about who has the greater number of soldiers and more advanced weapons. If it were, how could we explain America losing a war to North Vietnam? Although we won virtually every battle, we lost that war—at home.

Recently we've seen a burgeoning antiwar movement, reminiscent of that during the 1960s Vietnam era. Back then, widespread opposition to the Vietnam War was fueled by overtly leftist and even communist groups, whose efforts were multiplied by the news media, which opposed the war. The same phenomenon is happening today, including the far left and communist groups at the forefront. And the same terrible outcome is possible, if America loses its courage in this war. Only this time it would be much worse: No one was worrying about the North Vietnamese slipping across America's borders to detonate nuclear bombs or launch a biological weapons terror attack. But with our current enemy, that is this nation's No. 1 concern.

Make no mistake, the leaders and organizers of current antiwar demonstrations, like the giant one in Washington, D.C., in September [2005], are groups openly aligned with terrorist and communist regimes—groups like ANSWER, which the Washington Post described as "one of the main antiwar groups coordinating" the rally in the nation's capital. The Post didn't see fit to mention that ANSWER ("Act Now to Stop War and End Racism") is just a front group for the ultra-leftist Workers World Party, which enthusiastically supports North Korea and other dangerous, wacko regimes, and even worse—supports the "Iraqi resistance" which is killing American troops in Iraq.

Like Vietnam, the lraq War is controversial. There are valid, honest and compelling arguments both for and against this war—that is, over whether we should have taken the terror war to that location in the first place.

However, there are few or no compelling arguments for abandoning the fight now that we are there. Virtually everyone, except the most radical appeaser, recognizes it would be disastrous to "cut and run," which would widely be perceived as a monumental victory for terrorism. It would undoubtedly fuel a new and much larger round of radical jihad recruiting and the violence that inevitably follows.

Fifteen years from now, the Iraq War may be considered to have been a mistake. Or it may be regarded by historians to have been strategically brilliant and visionary to have planted and nurtured a relatively free, democratic country right in the heart of the Arab-Muslim Middle East, in between "axis of evil" countries Iran and Syria. Time will tell.

But what is indisputable is that Islamic radicalism is very, very real, and is intent on 1) dominating the entire Middle East, 2) wiping Israel off the map, and later, 3) fulfilling what it sees as its mission of bringing the entire world into a state of submission to the religion of Muhammad. It's already happening in Europe.

Losing the Battle for Hearts and Minds

This global jihad can succeed only if we lose the battle for hearts and minds—our own. Consider well the words attributed to Ayman al-Zawahiri, [al Qaeda leader] Osama bin Laden's chief lieutenant, in his recent July 9 [2005] letter (captured by U.S. troops) to al-Qaida's top leader in Iraq, Abu Musab al-Zarqawi. Despite claims by al-Qaida that it's a forgery, the U.S. government says it "has the highest confidence in the letter's authenticity."

". . . I say to you that we are in a battle," Bin Laden's No. 2 man says to his Iraqi commander, "and that more than half of this battle is taking place in the battlefield of the media. And that we are in a media battle in a race for the hearts and minds of our Umma [worldwide Muslim community]. And that however far our capabilities reach, they will never be equal to one-thousandth of the capabilities of the kingdom of Satan that is waging war on us."

In other words, although their military capabilities "will never be equal to one-thousandth of the capabilities" of America, they can still win. How?

During the 1960s, the antiwar movement, driven by profoundly anti-American groups—whose efforts were legitimized and multiplied by the news media—ultimately caused America to lose its courage and lose the war. What do you think? Is the same thing happening now? And isn't that exactly what our Islamo-fascist enemies would love most?

8

The United States Must Tolerate Islamism

Robin Wright

A distinguished journalist who has written for the New Yorker, Foreign Affairs, *and the* Los Angeles Times, *Robin Wright is currently the diplomatic correspondent for the* Washington Post. *She is also the author of* Sacred Rage: The Wrath of Militant Islam *and* The Last Great Revolution: Turmoil and Transformation in Iran.

The United States will not defeat radical Islam through military means, and the country cannot hope to overturn the nationalist philosophies that drive Islamism by appealing to the moderate Muslims because they are too small of a group to make large social changes. Instead, the United States and its allies must accept that Islamism will be part of world affairs and begin incorporating Islamists into the political process that will shape the future. Doing so will appease Islamists' hostility and likely rob them of their fundamentalist zeal to oppose all things that are not part of Islam.

Psychologists say the most intense period of mourning lasts three years. Since Sept. 11, 2001, Americans have indeed passed through several stages of grief, from disbelief to anger to a degree of acceptance. Yet, there's still a gnawing fear in our bellies that prevents full recovery. It's a fear that extends, I believe, well beyond [al Qaeda terrorist leader] Osama bin Laden and the prospects of another attack, and centers instead on our relationship with Islam itself.

Once familiar to most Americans mainly from seventh grade social studies, Islam has now become synonymous in the minds of many with the biggest post-Cold War threat. Even as we struggle to understand it, we're afraid of it. And because of that fear, we're drawing a Green Curtain around the Muslim world, creating an enduring divide.

Figuring out Islam's role in the 21st century is an existential challenge, but one many of us are emotionally unprepared to face. We pretend that we're not prejudiced, that we understand that most Muslims don't support the horrific bloodshed of bin Ladenism. Yet we still view 1.2 billion Muslim people spread throughout 53 countries as a threatening monolith. As long as we make that mistake, America and its allies won't feel safe, no matter how many billions of dollars are poured into security precautions.

Aside from the vital mission of tracking down bin Ladenists, military muscle is not always an effective instrument for moving forward. Nor are tepid diplomatic initiatives aimed at coaxing authoritarian governments into adopting change at a pace and in a manner that they control. There's another strategy that's gaining favor among Mideast experts: Bring Islamic movements and groups into the political process. Give Islamist parties new political space—wide open space—to absorb passions and sap anger.

[A]lienation—from closed political systems and corrupt economies—is what originally drove many Muslims to seek refuge in their mosques.

Working with Islamists

That means accepting, even embracing, the idea that Islam is not the problem, but the way out of a political predicament that has been building quietly for decades. It means not only supporting nationalists, liberals and nascent democrats already on our side in the quest to transform the Middle East but also encouraging Islamists and their parties to participate. Basically, it means differentiating between Islamists and jihadists, and accepting anyone willing to work within a system to change it rather than work from outside to destroy it.

"It's hard to imagine political evolution in the next 20 years that does not include the Islamists," says Ellen Laipson, president of the Stimson Center, a Washington think tank that studies international security issues. "They have established legitimacy and a following and you won't make them disappear overnight by supporting the activities of a small elite of secular modernists. . . . You have to imagine a political space that has both."

Mideast scholars say it's too late to do anything less. The alternative is alienating even more Muslims by excluding them. And alienation—from closed political systems and corrupt economies—is what originally drove many Muslims to seek refuge in their mosques.

Including Islamists in government is an uncomfortable idea for those of us in secular societies. It summons up haunting images of Iranian clerics and American hostages, oppressed women and antiquated laws. That's why for years, U.S. governments have accepted Algeria's military, which voided free elections won by Islamic parties, and Hosni Mubarak's suppression of Egypt's Muslim groups. That's shortsighted because perpetuating the status quo will be worse. Now that Islamists have moved from the fringe to the center of political activity, a trend that has accelerated since the U.S. invasion of Iraq, they can no longer be excluded.

Moving Beyond War Mentality

We have to think outside the prism of the war on terrorism. "Even as it wages a resolute campaign against international terrorism, America should not believe that it is engaged in a fight to the finish with radical Islam," Robert Hutchings, chairman of the National Intelligence Council, wrote in a recent [2004] issue of *Foreign Policy* magazine. "This conflict is not a clash of civilizations, but rather a defense of our shared humanity and a search for common ground, however implausible that may seem now."

One of the hopeful signs on this third anniversary of 9/11 is the way Americans are emerging from their grief to discuss a more creative course for the future and to more effectively answer the lingering question: What *can* America do? A growing number of voices on both the right and the left have been emboldened to shape proposals in a broader context.

The United States has tipped its hat to political change with initiatives to promote democracy. As President [George W.] Bush said in a June [2004] speech in Istanbul, "Democratic societies should welcome, not fear, the participation of the faithful."

Yet in practice, the United States still veers away from Islamists. In Iraq, which Washington seeks to turn into a model for the region, U.N. and U.S. envoys deliberately picked politicians mainly from secular parties to assume power after the formal end of the U.S.-led occupation. Despite strong support in opinion polls, Islamist parties were marginalized. Analysts now predict they'll make a comeback in next year's elections and the United States would be wise not to try to prevent it.

Attempts to control the pace of change or choose the participants in the political process could invite an even deeper backlash than we face now.

"Political debate must encompass Islam if the debate is to be meaningful. Exclusion of the Islamic factor in Arab politics will simply be one-sided and unrealistic in its exclusion of the single greatest force within politics," writes Graham Fuller, a former senior intelligence analyst, in a paper released this month by the Carnegie Endowment for International Peace.

The same applies to the wider Islamic world that constitutes 18 percent of the world's people.

Fundamentalism Will Burn Itself Out

In the race to capture the imagination of the vast, alienated middle, hard-line groups need to be operating under the same legal umbrella as more moderate groups—or they will try to lure the faithful through other means. "It's hard to hand over individual authority to people who are illiberal. What you have to realize is that the objective is to defeat bin Ladenism and you have to start the evolution. Moderate Muslims are not the answer. Shiite clerics and Sunni fundamentalists are our salvation from future 9/11s," says Reuel Marc Gerecht, a Middle East expert and senior fellow at the American Enterprise Institute.

Transitions away from authoritarian regimes may be messier and more volatile than political transformations elsewhere over the past quarter century. But "Let it roll," Gerecht advises. "Don't walk away. It's part of the process. It's trying to ensure the system is sufficiently open that fundamentalists burn themselves out. You have to rob bin Ladenism of that virulent elixir. If we don't go in that direction, we know all other roads go back to 9/11."

"You want in a Machiavellian way to have fundamentalists do the dirty work," he says. "You want them to take care of the people who slaughtered the children [in Beslan, Russia, September 2004]. The only way to do that is to have them compete in the political system. It may come off the rails for a while in some places, but even if it does, you will be better off. You don't want fundamentalists to take states by coups d'etat."

The premise behind the new ideas is that activists inspired or protected by religion have stood in for jailed or exiled secular opposition figures in many societies. "Rebellion to tyrants is obedience to God," Benjamin Franklin once said. And more recently, liberation theologians in Latin America, Jewish refuseniks in the Soviet Union, South Africa's Anglican Archbishop Desmond Tutu and Catholic priests in Poland and the Philippines have played pivotal roles in political transformations.

"Conservative and even fundamentalist views of religion are manageable in a plural environment, as shown by a host of Protestant, Catholic and Jewish cases," wrote French scholar Olivier Roy in the new anthology *A Practical Guide to Winning the War on Terrorism.* "A pluralist approach allows civil society to reach the cadres of youth who could be ideal targets for radicals and neo-fundamentalist groups."

Attempts to control the pace of change or choose the participants in the political process could invite an even deeper backlash than we face now. America cannot want less for Muslim countries than it wants for the rest of the world. And Muslims must not feel they are bystanders. "In the end, you have to treat Muslims as adults. They have to become responsible for their own fate," says Gerecht.

The United States Must Start a Dialogue with Islamists

Based on conversations with Mideast experts, it appears that in the meantime, the United States could do three things. First, hold a genuine two-way dialogue. For all the hand-wringing about ending hatreds, that essential element is missing.

In a speech at the U.S. Institute of Peace [in August 2004], national security adviser Condoleezza Rice said that the United States must do more with the Islamic world to dispel "destructive myths" about America and to support "voices of moderation." The most striking thing about the speech was that she gave it to an American audience. Asked why no senior U.S. official had given a similar speech in any of the five largest Muslim countries in the three years since Sept. 11, she replied, "That's a good question. Maybe we should."

Dialogue must not just engage people listed in the local U.S. embassy's Rolodex. We need to listen to the bad guys too to understand where the fissures—and opportunities—might be.

"Even the hard-core jihadis are having big debates about who exactly the enemy is and . . . about their tactics," says Princeton University Mideast expert Michael Doran, who gets up early each morning to research Islamist and jihadi Web sites. When U.S. contractor Paul Johnson was beheaded in Saudi Arabia "some said it was wrong. Others said, 'Our violence makes us look bad.' One of the most important ideologues, Abu Baseer, a cleric who was an Afghan jihadist, said 'Westerners in our society have protection.' The radicals countered that an apostate state—Saudi Arabia—can't grant immunity. But Baseer said, 'That's not right, we haven't thrown traditions out.' Three years after Sept. 11 . . . the debate among them is totally unknown."

A second course of U.S. action would be to use economic tools. Several Muslim countries, including Algeria, Lebanon, Saudi Arabia, Yemen, Libya, Iran and Iraq, are seeking membership in the World Trade Organization [WTO]. The United States could use WTO membership to induce change and force countries to embrace the rule of law.

Finally, we can embrace our own Islamic identity. Islam, the fastest-growing religion in the United States, is expected to become the second-largest faith in six years. Yet Muslims remain on the fringe. Just ask women who cover their heads or men with beards waiting in the boarding areas of airports.

Immediately after 9/11, Bush visited the Islamic Center in Washington and said Islam was not the enemy. This is a noble sentiment, but Muslims must also become part of the mainstream—a challenge faced throughout the West. For Europeans, the most important battle for Muslim hearts and minds over the next decade will not be fought in the Middle East but in European cities where the numbers of Muslims are growing, as Giles Kepel, a French expert on Islam, says in his new book *The War for Muslim Minds: Islam and the West*. "If European societies are able to integrate these Muslim populations . . . this new generation of Muslims may become the Islamic vanguard of the next decade," he writes.

The unspoken undercurrent behind our failure to do more over the past three years is what former national security adviser Zbigniew Brzezinski calls "a fear that periodically verges on panic that is in itself blind." As we look beyond our grief, we must also get beyond our prejudice and fear.

9

Islam Oppresses Women

Azam Kamguian

Azam Kamguian is an Iranian writer and women's rights activist. She is the editor of the Bulletin of the Committee to Defend Women's Rights in the Middle East.

Islam as a religion, culture, and political force has traditionally deprived women of their rights and made them second-class citizens in nations that are governed by Islamic law. The oppression has been most keenly felt after the rise of political Islam in the 1970s. In the decades that followed, Muslim women have lived as virtual slaves and prisoners, restricted in the jobs they can hold, the education they can attain, and the rights they possess. The only hope for women's liberation in Muslim countries is to depose political Islam and create secular states that respect the rights of all citizens.

Women's status in Middle Eastern societies has aroused great interest recently. What role do Islamic ideology and practice play in the oppression of women in the region and other societies where Islam holds sway?

Few would argue that the situation of Middle Eastern women can be understood without reference to Islam. Although no two Middle Eastern countries have identical legal-religious systems, women are second-class citizens in all of them. But the position of women in the region cannot be un-

Azam Kamguian, "Islam and the Liberation of Women in the Middle East: Separation of Mosque and State is the Only Answer," *Free Inquiry*, vol. 23, October–November 2003. Reproduced by permission.

derstood without a thorough appreciation of the economic and political contexts in which they live, in addition to Islam's long-standing influence.

There are many schools of thought in this debate. One group denies that the great majority of women are any more oppressed than are non-Middle Eastern women. A second group says that oppression is real but extrinsic to Islam and the Qur'an—which, they say, intended gender equality but has been undermined by Arabic patriarchy and foreign influence.

Among intellectuals and in the academic world, any attempt to blame Islam for women's oppression is stamped as Orientalism. Those who defend Islam against Western critiques focus on proving the "progressive" nature of the Qur'an, Hadith [tales of the words and deeds of the prophet Muhammad], and Sharia [Islamic law], either by denying the low status of women in Middle Eastern societies, or by attributing it to pre-Islamic traditions and the contemporary political Islamic movement.

In Iran, the Sudan, Pakistan, and Afghanistan under the Taliban, Islamic regimes transformed societies in general and women's homes in particular into prisons.

Many feminists and academic intellectuals apologize for Islam by saying that such practices as veiling women and female genital mutilation are not restricted to Middle Eastern societies. Some say that women who wear make-up in the West are just as oppressed, but it is a Postmodernist, neo-colonialist kind of oppression. They say that all religions regard women as inferior. They fail to take into account that Islam is largely unrestricted by secularism and the secular states that in the West have restricted Christianity's power over women's lives. This attitude is obvious in the following words of [the Egyptian feminist writer] Nawal El Saadawi:

I've noticed that many people including professors of religion and Islamic studies, pick up one verse and say that in the Qur'an, God allowed men to beat women. They don't compare it to other verses. They also don't compare the Qur'an to the Bible. If you do, you will find the Bible more oppressive to women.

According to El Saadawi, women in the Middle East are oppressed not because they live under the rule of Islam or belong to the East, but as a result of the patriarchal class system that has dominated the world for thousands of years. In her view, the struggle for women's civil liberties, individual freedom, and secularism have no significance. In this discourse, patriarchy is used as a blanket term to disguise Islam's role in the oppression of women. Every aspect of women's subordination in the Middle East is inaccurately labeled as the result of patriarchy. If Islam has no effect on women's status, why is the position of women in the Middle East worse than in any other part of the world?

Islamic Resistance to Women's Rights

Historically, Islam has resisted women's rights, secularism, and modernization. Dramatic differences between the East and non-Muslim West emerged in the nineteenth and twentieth centuries. Economic and social changes, along with the impact of exposure to Western culture, gave rise to forces within Middle Eastern societies that favored changes in the condition of women. Starting in the early nineteenth century, the process of change set in motion by Western influence led to broadly positive outcomes, as mechanisms for controlling women and excluding them from major domains of activity in their society were gradually dismantled.

At first this didn't involve legal changes, but rather such things as education. Western economic penetration of the Middle East and the exposure of Middle Eastern societies to Western political thought and ideas did little to dismantle either Islamic law or the backward social institutions oppressive to women. Changes in Islamic law pertaining to women, especially changes to law set forth in the Qur'an, have met with considerable resistance. The leaders of nationalistic factions viewed any proposed changes in the status of women in society as Western intrusion into their last sphere of control. They had already seen Western inroads upon their sovereignty and their economies. Islamists saw modern values such as women's rights as a Western conspiracy accompanying the political and economic offensive and turned to their own traditions as a cultural reaction. For an early example, when Napoleon came to Egypt, the wearing of the veil increased as a reaction to the French presence.

If Islam has no effect on women's status, why is the position of women in the Middle East worse than in any other part of the world?

Men were prominent in the early struggles to improve the condition of women in Islamic society, but from the beginning women, too, were involved. For the first time in the history of Islam, the veil and other issues such as polygamy, divorce, and segregation were openly discussed in Middle Eastern society. Advocacy for women's rights became widespread in the twentieth century. Modernization further improved women's position. As women's economic and social situation improved, ideologues struggled with how to reconcile the changes with Islamic law. Women figured more prominently in public life and took a role in the history-making nation building of Turkey and Tunisia, which led to further secularization and economic modernization.

But establishment Islam and Middle Eastern governments continue to cling to the law as the cornerstone of Islamic oppression of women. That it is still preserved almost intact signals the existence of enormously powerful Islamist and traditionalist forces. Calls for reformist interpretations such as stressing the "egalitarian spirit of the Qur'an" and reshaping Sharia by reinterpreting the Qur'an mainly arose because of a rapidly changing economy and society experiencing the influence of the West. Legal reforms have targeted areas where the law was not egalitarian, such as divorce, polygamy, and marriage age. Some progress has been made: men must now justify their demand for divorce or practice of polygamy to the courts.

By failing to protect women from violence such as domestic abuse, rape, marital rape, and honor killing, the state fails to provide the rights available to a full citizen.

Political Islam's Anti-Progressive Views

In recent decades the rise of political Islam has rolled back women's rights and impoverished their lives across the region. Political Islam as a political movement arose in reaction to secular and progressive liberation movements, which had heightened egalitarianism and brought about cultural and intellectual advances. The political Islamic movement started to gather real power and to spread in the 1970s. During the 1980s it was supported and nurtured by Western governments, which found it useful in Cold War conflicts and in opposing progressive movements in the region. Key features of political Islam included opposition to women's freedom and civil liberties, and to their freedom of expression in the cultural and personal domains. It supports the enforcement of brutal laws and traditions, including beheading and genocide. In Iran, the Sudan, Pakistan, and Afghanistan under the Taliban, Islamic regimes transformed societies in general and women's homes in particular into prisons. For women confinement, exclusion from many fields of work and education, and brutal treatment became the law of the land. In addition, the misogynist rhetoric of political Islam in the social sphere implicitly sanctioned male violence towards women.

Women Lack Full Citizenship

At present, women throughout the region are second-class citizens, being excluded from the rights, privileges, and security that all citizens of a country should enjoy. Unjust laws, discriminatory constitutions, and biased mentalities that do not recognize women as equal citizens violate women's rights. A national, that is, a citizen, is defined as someone who is a native or naturalized member of a state. A national is entitled to the rights and privileges allotted to a free individual and to protection from the state. However, in no country in the Middle East or Northern Africa are women granted full citizenship; in every country they are second-class citizens. In many cases, the laws and codes of the state work to reinforce gender inequality and exclusion from nationality. The state is used to strengthen Islamic and tribal/familial control over women, making them even more dependent on these institutions. Unlike in the West, where the individual is the basic unit of the state, it is the family that is the basis of Arab states. This means that the state is primarily concerned with the protection of the family rather than the protection of the family's individual members. Within this framework, the rights of women are expressed solely in their roles as wives and mothers. State discrimination against women in the family is expressed through, among other things, unjust family laws that deny women equal access to divorce and child custody.

Throughout the region, Arab women who marry foreigners are denied the right to extend citizenship to their husbands. Furthermore only fathers, not mothers, can independently pass citizenship to their children. In many cases, where a woman has been widowed, divorced, or abandoned, or if her husband is not a national in the country where the couple reside, her children have no access to citizenship or its rights.

These rights include access to education, health care, land ownership, and inheritance. There is no such obstacle to men who wish to extend their nationality to their wives and children. This inequality not only denies women their right as citizens; it also denies children their basic rights as human beings.

The Law Does Not Protect Women

If the law is designed to protect women only within their role in the family, it will fail to protect those who need protection from their families. By failing to protect women from violence such as domestic abuse, rape, marital rape, and honor killing, the state fails to provide the rights available to a full citizen. In fact, by ignoring issues of gender-based violence and granting lenient punishments to the perpetrators of violence against women, the state actually reinforces women's exclusion from the rights of citizens.

Family laws based on Sharia frequently require women to obtain a male relative's permission to undertake activities that should be theirs by right. This increases the dependency women have on their male family members in economic, social, and legal matters. For example, in many Arab countries adult women must obtain the permission of their fathers, brothers, or husbands in order to attain a passport, travel outside of their country, start a business, receive a bank loan, open a bank account, or get married.

Political Islam Must Be Abolished

Given Islam's intrinsic animosity to equality between the sexes, to women's rights, and toward women's roles in society, how can the condition of women in Islamic societies be improved? The answer must be to eliminate political Islam as a precondition to any improvements in the status of women in the Middle East. The social system is based on Islamic misogyny and backwardness, and Middle Eastern women will have no cause to regret its passing.

The twenty-first century must be the century that rids itself of political Islam. I believe that this movement will begin in Iran. In Iran, women presented the first and the most effective challenge to the Islamic regime by courageously questioning the right of Islamic authority to define the conditions of their lives. The most hopeful signs and the most remarkable force for change continue to come directly from Iranian women, both in Iran and in exile.

As ever, the key to Middle Eastern women's liberation is secularism and the establishment of egalitarian political systems. Secularism has been and continues to be a prerequisite for women's liberation in the Middle East. Our objectives must be:

- the complete separation of religion from the state;

- the elimination of all religious and religiously inspired concepts from laws;

- definition of religion as the private affair of individuals;

- removal of references to a person's religion in laws, on identity cards, and in official papers;

- a ban on ascribing any religion to people, whether individually or collectively, in official documents and the media;

- elimination of religion from education; and

- a ban on teaching religious subjects and dogma and on presenting purely religious interpretations of secular subjects in schools.

Why should Islam be eliminated from the operations of the state instead of modernized and reformed? If someone says that slavery, fascism, or patriarchy can become humane and modernized, I would ask them why they should not be abandoned altogether. In the view of advocates of Islamic reform, if Islam allowed a woman to go to school in a knee-length skirt or to become a judge as long as she does not speak of her sexuality, then it would be acceptable. This is not the improvement that we deserve. Attempts to modernize or reform Islam will only prolong the age-old oppression and subordination of women. Rather than modernize Islam, it must be caged, just as humanity caged Christianity two centuries ago. Islam must become subordinate to secularism and the secular state.

10

Islam Does Not Oppress Women

Ruqaiyyah Waris Maqsood

Ruqaiyyah Waris Maqsood grew up a devout Christian but converted to Islam in 1986. She was the head of religious studies at various secondary schools in the United Kingdom until her retirement in 1996. She is the author of over forty books on Islam and other subjects.

Islamic culture is definitely patriarchal, but Muslim women are not its victims. Rather, Islamic law recognizes the equality of women in many matters and prescribes set roles for women and men for the benefit of family life. Muslim men are expected to treat their wives well, and they cannot engage in capricious behavior that would threaten the sacred marriage union. Wives are expected to accept their husbands as the head of their households, but women are not obligated to share their own property or relinquish their work salary to their husbands or to obey any command that defies the will of God. In fact, wives have control of much of their household environment and can obtain a divorce if problems arise.

How can anyone justify Islam's treatment of women, when it imprisons Afghans under blue shuttlecock burqas and makes Pakistani girls marry strangers against their will?

How can you respect a religion that forces women into polygamous marriages, mutilates their genitals, forbids them to drive cars and subjects them to the humiliation of "instant" divorce? In fact, none of these practices are Islamic at all.

Ruqaiyyah Waris Maqsood, "Islam, Culture and Women," *Islam for Today*. Reproduced by permission. www.islamfortoday.com.

Anyone wishing to understand Islam must first separate the religion from the cultural norms and style of a society. Female genital mutilation is still practised in certain pockets of Africa and Egypt, but viewed as an inconceivable horror by the vast majority of Muslims. Forced marriages may still take place in certain Indian, Pakistani and Bangladeshi communities, but would be anathema to Muslim women from other backgrounds.

Indeed, Islam insists on the free consent of both bride and groom, so such marriages could even be deemed illegal under religious law.

The Koran is addressed to all Muslims, and for the most part it does not differentiate between male and female.

Cultural Prohibitions, Not Islamic Prohibitions

A woman forbidden from driving a car in Riyadh will cheerfully take the wheel when abroad, confident that her country's bizarre law has nothing to do with Islam. Afghan women educated before the Taliban rule know that banning girls from school is forbidden in Islam, which encourages all Muslims to seek knowledge from cradle to grave, from every source possible.

The Koran is addressed to all Muslims, and for the most part it does not differentiate between male and female. Man and woman, it says, "were created of a single soul," and are moral equals in the sight of God. Women have the right to divorce, to inherit property, to conduct business and to have access to knowledge.

Since women are under all the same obligations and rules of conduct as the men, differences emerge most strongly when it comes to pregnancy, child-bearing and rearing, menstruation and, to a certain extent, clothing.

Some of the commands are alien to Western tradition. Requirements of ritual purity may seem to restrict a woman's access to religious life, but are viewed as concessions. During menstruation or postpartum bleeding, she may not pray the ritual salah or touch the Koran and she does not have to fast; nor does she need to fast while pregnant or nursing.

Dress and Marriage Restrictions

The veiling of Muslim women is a more complex issue. Certainly, the Koran requires them to behave and dress modestly—but these strictures apply equally to men. Only one verse refers to the veiling of women, stating that the Prophet's wives should be behind a hijab when his male guests converse with them.

Some modernists, however, claim that this does not apply to women in general, and that the language used does not carry the textual stipulation that makes a verse obligatory. In practice, most modern Muslim women appreciate attractive and graceful clothes, but avoid dressing provocatively.

Contrary to Christianity, Islam does not regard marriages as "made in heaven" or "till death do us part". They are contracts, with conditions.

What about polygamy, which the Koran endorses up to the limit of four wives per man? The Prophet, of course, lived at a time when continual warfare produced large numbers of widows, who were left with little or no provision for themselves and their children.

In these circumstances, polygamy was encouraged as an act of charity. Needless to say, the widows were not necessarily sexy young women, but usually mothers of up to six children, who came as part of the deal.

Polygamy is no longer common, for various good reasons. The Koran states that wives need to be treated fairly and equally—a difficult requirement even for a rich man. More-over, if a husband wishes to take a second wife, he should not do so if the marriage will be to the detriment of the first.

Adultery and Divorce

Sexual intimacy outside marriage is forbidden in Islam, in-cluding sex before marriage, adultery or homosexual relation-ships. However, within marriage, sexual intimacy should be raised from the animal level to sadaqah (a form of worship) so that each considers the happiness and satisfaction of the other, rather than mere self-gratification.

Contrary to Christianity, Islam does not regard marriages as "made in heaven" or "till death do us part". They are con-tracts, with conditions. If either side breaks the conditions, di-vorce is not only allowed, but usually expected. Nevertheless, a hadith makes it clear that: "Of all the things God has allowed, divorce is the most disliked."

[A woman's] husband is not her master; a Muslim woman has only one Master, and that is God.

A Muslim has a genuine reason for divorce only if a spouse's behaviour goes against the sunnah of Islam—in other words, if he or she has become cruel, vindictive, abusive, un-faithful, neglectful, selfish, sexually abusive, tyrannical, per-verted—and so on.

In good Islamic practice, before divorce can be contem-plated, all possible efforts should be made to solve a couple's problems. After an intention to divorce is announced, there is a three-month period during which more attempts are made at reconciliation.

If, by the end of each month, the couple have resumed sexual intimacy, the divorce should not proceed. The three-month rule ensures that a woman cannot remarry until three menstrual cycles have passed—so, if she happens to be pregnant, the child will be supported and paternity will not be in dispute.

When Muslims die, strict laws govern the shares of property and money they may leave to others; daughters usually inherit less than sons, but this is because the men in a family are supposed to provide for the entire household.

The Roles of Wives and Husbands

Any money or property owned by women is theirs to keep, and they are not obliged to share it. Similarly, in marriage, a woman's salary is hers and cannot be appropriated by her husband unless she consents.

A good Muslim woman, for her part, should always be trustworthy and kind. She should strive to be cheerful and encouraging towards her husband and family, and keep their home free from anything harmful (haram covers all aspects of harm, including bad behaviour, abuse and forbidden foods).

Regardless of her skills or intelligence, she is expected to accept her man as the head of her household—she must, therefore, take care to marry a man she can respect, and whose wishes she can carry out with a clear conscience. However, when a man expects his wife to do anything contrary to the will of God—in other words, any nasty, selfish, dishonest or cruel action—she has the right to refuse him.

Her husband is not her master; a Muslim woman has only one Master, and that is God. If her husband does not represent God's will in the home, the marriage contract is broken.

What should one make of the verse in the Koran that allows a man to punish his wife physically? There are important provisos: he may do so only if her ill-will is wrecking the marriage—but then only after he has exhausted all attempts at verbal communication and tried sleeping in a separate bed.

However, the Prophet never hit a woman, child or old person, and was emphatic that those who did could hardly regard themselves as the best of Muslims. Moreover, he also stated that a man should never hit "one of God's handmaidens". Nor, it must be said, should wives beat their husbands or become inveterate nags.

Finally, there is the issue of giving witness. Although the Koran says nothing explicit, other Islamic sources suggest that a woman's testimony in court is worth only half of that of a man. This ruling, however, should be applied only in circumstances where a woman is uneducated and has led a very restricted life: a woman equally qualified to a man will carry the same weight as a witness.

Men and Women Are Moral Equals

So, does Islam oppress women?

While the spirit of Islam is clearly patriarchal, it regards men and women as moral equals. Moreover, although a man is technically the head of the household, Islam encourages matriarchy in the home.

Women may not be equal in the manner defined by Western feminists, but their core differences from men are acknowledged, and they have rights of their own that do not apply to men.

11

Islam Is Compatible with Democracy

Reza Aslan

Born in Iran, Reza Aslan is a writer and scholar of religions and serves as a commentator for National Public Radio's Marketplace program and a Middle East Analyst for CBS News. He is also the author of No God but God: The Origins, Evolution, and Future of Islam.

Many commentators in the West believe that Islam and democracy can never cohere because of Islamic fundamentalist governments' foregrounding of religious dogma at the expense of secular interests; however, democracy is defined by pluralism—the tolerance of diverse opinions—and Islamic nations have traditionally shown an acceptance of multi-ethnic, multi-religious populations. While strict fundamentalist thinking has dampened the democratic spirit in many Islamic countries today, the tolerance for pluralism that is inherent in Islam suggests that reform movements advocating greater secularization will eventually purge Arab nations of the religious fanaticism that currently holds sway.

Almost immediately following the [terrorist] attacks on New York and Washington, pundits, politicians, and preachers throughout the United States and Europe declared that September 11, 2001, had triggered a once-dormant "clash of civilizations" between the modern, enlightened, democratic societies of the West and the archaic, barbarous, autocratic so-

Reza Aslan, "From Islam, Pluralist Democracies Will Surely Grow," from *No God but God*. Copyright © 2005 by Reza Aslan. Used by permission of Random House.

cieties of the Middle East. A few well-respected academics carried that argument further by suggesting that the failure of
democracy to emerge in the Muslim world was due in large
part to Muslim culture, which they claimed was intrinsically
incompatible with such Enlightenment values as liberalism,
pluralism, individualism, and human rights.

Just beneath the surface of that misguided and divisive
rhetoric is a more subtle, though far more detrimental, sentiment: that this is not so much a cultural conflict as a religious
one; that we are not in the midst of a clash of civilizations,
but rather a clash of monotheisms.

[There is] a rapidly growing movement of Christian missionaries who, since September 11, have begun to focus exclu-
sively on the Muslim world. Because Christian evangelism is
often bitterly reproached in Muslim countries—thanks in
large part to the lingering memory of the colonial endeavor,
when Europe's disastrous "civilizing mission" went hand in
hand with a fervently anti-Islamic "Christianizing mission"—
some evangelical institutions now teach their missionaries to
"go undercover" in the Muslim world by taking on Muslim
identities, wearing Muslim clothing (including the veil), even
fasting and praying as Muslims.

---

*Religion is, by definition, interpretation; and by defini-
tion, all interpretations are valid.*

At the same time, the U.S. government has encouraged
large numbers of Christian aid organizations to take an active
role in rebuilding the infrastructures of Iraq and Afghanistan
in the wake of the two wars, giving ammunition to those who
seek to portray the occupation of those countries as a re-
newed crusade of Christians against Muslims. Add to that the
perception, held by many in the Muslim world, that there is
collusion between the United States and Israel against Muslim
interests in general and Palestinian rights in particular, and

one can understand how Muslims' resentment and suspicion of the West has only increased, and with disastrous consequences.

Gaining an Appreciation of Islam

Considering how effortlessly religious dogma has become intertwined with political ideology since September 11, how can we overcome the clash-of-monotheisms mentality that has so deeply entrenched itself in the modern world? Clearly, education and tolerance are essential. But what is most desperately needed is not so much a better appreciation of our neighbor's religion as a broader, more complete understanding of religion itself.

Religion, it must be understood, is not faith. Religion is the story of faith. It is an institutionalized system of symbols and metaphors (read: rituals and myths) that provides a common language with which members of a community of faith can share with each other their numinous encounter with the Divine Presence. Religion is concerned not with genuine history but with sacred history, which does not course through time like a river.

Rather, sacred history is like a hallowed tree whose roots dig deep into primordial time and whose branches weave in and out of genuine history with little concern for the boundaries of space and time. Indeed, it is precisely at those moments when sacred and genuine history collide that religions are born. The clash of monotheisms occurs when faith, which is mysterious and ineffable and which eschews all categorizations, becomes entangled in the gnarled branches of religion.

The story of Islam is anchored in the memories of the first generation of Muslims and cataloged by the Prophet Muhammad's earliest biographers, Ibn Ishaq (d. 768), Ibn Hisham (d. 833), and al-Tabari (d. 922). At the heart of the story is the Glorious Quran—the divine revelations that Muhammad received during a span of some 26 years in Mecca and Medina. While the Quran tells us very little about Muhammad's life (indeed, he is rarely mentioned), it is invaluable in revealing the ideology of the Muslim faith in its infancy: that is, before the faith became a religion, before the religion became an institution.

Various Strands of Islam

Religion is, by definition, interpretation; and by definition, all interpretations are valid. However, some interpretations are more reasonable than others. And as the Jewish philosopher and mystic Moses Maimonides noted so many years ago, it is reason, not imagination, that determines what is probable and what is not.

Considering how often Islam has been used to rationalize the brutal policies of oppressive totalitarian regimes . . . it is hardly surprising that the term "Islamic democracy" provokes such skepticism in the West.

The way scholars form a reasonable interpretation of a particular religious tradition is by merging that religion's myths with what can be known about the spiritual and political landscape in which those myths arose. By relying on the Quran and the traditions of the Prophet, along with our understanding of the cultural milieu in which Muhammad was born and in which his message was formed, we can more reasonably reconstruct the origins and evolution of Islam.

It is possible to trace how Muhammad's revolutionary message of moral accountability and social egalitarianism was gradually reinterpreted by his successors into competing ideologies of rigid legalism and uncompromising orthodoxy, which fractured the Muslim community and widened the gap between mainstream, or Sunni, Islam and its two major sectarian movements, Shiism and Sufism. Although sharing a common sacred history, each group strove to develop its own interpretation of scripture, its own ideas on theology and the law, and its own community of faith. And each had different responses to the experience of colonialism in the 18th and 19th centuries.

Indeed, that experience forced the entire Muslim community to reconsider the role of faith in modern society. While some Muslims pushed for the creation of an indigenous Islamic Enlightenment by eagerly developing Islamic alternatives to Western secular notions of democracy, others advocated separation from Western cultural ideals in favor of the complete "Islamization" of society. With the end of colonialism and the birth of the Islamic state, in the 20th century, those two groups have refined their arguments against the backdrop of the continuing debate in the Muslim world over the prospect of forming a genuine Islamic democracy. But at the center of the debate over Islam and democracy is a far more significant internal struggle over who gets to define the Islamic Reformation that is already under way in most of the Muslim world.

Who Defines Islamic Democracy?

For most of the Western world, September 11, 2001, signaled the commencement of a worldwide struggle between Islam and the West—the ultimate manifestation of the clash of civilizations. From the Islamic perspective, however, the attacks on New York and Washington were part of a continuing clash between those Muslims who strive to reconcile their religious values with the realities of the modern world, and those who react to modernism and reform by reverting—sometimes fanatically—to the "fundamentals" of their faith.

Considering how often Islam has been used to rationalize the brutal policies of oppressive totalitarian regimes like the Taliban in Afghanistan, the Wahhabists in Saudi Arabia, and the Faqih in Iran, it is hardly surprising that the term "Islamic democracy" provokes such skepticism in the West. Some of the most celebrated academics in the United States and Europe reject the notion outright, believing that the principles of democracy cannot be reconciled with fundamental Islamic values. When politicians speak of bringing democracy to the Middle East, they mean specifically an American secular democracy, not an indigenous Islamic one.

It is pluralism, not secularism, that defines democracy.

There exists a philosophical dispute in the Western world with regard to the concept of Islamic democracy: that is, that there can be no a priori moral framework in a modern democracy; that the foundation of a genuinely democratic society must be secularism. The problem with that argument, however, is that it not only fails to recognize the inherently moral foundation upon which a large number of modern democracies are built, but also, more important, fails to appreciate the difference between secularism and secularization.

As the Protestant theologian Harvey Cox notes, secularization is the process by which "certain responsibilities pass from ecclesiastical to political authorities," whereas secularism is an ideology based on the eradication of religion from public life. Turkey is a secular country in which outward signs of religiosity, such as the hijab, are forcibly suppressed. With regard to ideological resolve, one could argue that there is little that separates a secular country like Turkey from a religious country like Iran; both ideologize society. The United States, however, is a secularizing country, unapologetically founded on a Judeo-Christian—and more precisely Protestant—moral framework.

One need only regard the language with which political issues like abortion rights and gay marriage are debated in Congress to recognize that religion is to this day an integral part of the American national identity and patently the moral foundation for its Constitution, its laws, and its national customs. Despite what school-children read in their history books, the reality is that the separation of church and state is not so much the foundation of American government as it is the result of a 250-year secularization process based not upon secularism, but upon pluralism.

Pluralism Is the Hallmark of Democracy

It is pluralism, not secularism, that defines democracy. A democratic state can be established upon any normative moral framework as long as pluralism remains the source of its legitimacy. Israel is founded upon an exclusivist Jewish moral framework that recognizes all the world's Jews—regardless of their nationality—as citizens of the state. England continues to maintain a national church whose religious head is also the country's sovereign. India was, until recently, governed by partisans of the elitist theology of Hindu Awakening (Hindutva), bent on applying their implausible but enormously successful vision of "true Hinduism" to the state. And yet, like the United States, those countries are all considered democracies, not because they are secular but because they are, at least in theory, dedicated to pluralism.

[R]eligious pluralism is the first step toward building an effective human-rights policy in the Middle East.

Islam has had a long commitment to religious pluralism. Muhammad's recognition of Jews and Christians as protected peoples (dhimmi), his belief in a common divine text from which all revealed scriptures are derived (the Umm al-Kitab), and his dream of establishing a single, united Ummah, encompassing all three faiths of Abraham, were startlingly revolutionary ideas in an era in which religion literally created borders between peoples. And despite the ways in which it has been interpreted by militants and fundamentalists who refuse to recognize its historical and cultural context, there are few scriptures in the great religions of the world that can match the reverence with which the Quran speaks of other religious traditions.

It is true that the Quran does not hold the same respect for polytheistic religions as it does for monotheistic ones. However, that is primarily a consequence of the fact that the Revelation was received during a protracted and bloody war with the "polytheistic" Quraysh, the ruling tribe of Mecca. The truth that is the Quranic designation of "protected peoples" was highly flexible and was routinely tailored to match public policy.

The foundation of Islamic pluralism can be summed up in one indisputable verse: "There can be no compulsion in religion." That means that the antiquated partitioning of the world into spheres of belief (dar al-Islam) and unbelief (dar al-Harb), which was first developed during the Crusades but which still maintains its grasp on the imaginations of traditionalist theologians, is utterly unjustifiable. It also means that the ideology of those Wahhabists who wish to return Islam to some imaginary ideal of original purity must be once and for all abandoned. Islam is and has always been a religion of diversity. The notion that there was once an original, unadulterated Islam that was shattered into heretical sects and schisms is a historical fiction. Both Shiism and Sufism in all their wonderful manifestations represent trends of thought that have existed from the very beginning of Islam, and both find their inspiration in the words and deeds of the Prophet. God may be One, but Islam most definitely is not.

Human Rights as a Religious Duty

Grounding an Islamic democracy in the ideals of pluralism is vital because religious pluralism is the first step toward building an effective human-rights policy in the Middle East. One need simply recall the Prophet's warning to those who questioned his egalitarian measures in Medina—"[They] will be thrown into Hell, where they will dwell forever, suffering from the most shameful punishment"—to recognize that acknowledging human rights in Islam is not simply a means of protecting civil liberties, it is a fundamental religious duty.

> *The function of the clergy in an Islamic democracy is not to rule, but to preserve and, more important, to reflect the morality of the state.*

Nevertheless, the Islamic vision of human rights is not a prescription for moral relativism. Nor does it imply freedom from ethical restraint. Islam's quintessentially communal character necessitates that any human-rights policy take into consideration the protection of the community over the autonomy of the individual. And while there may be some circumstances in which Islamic morality may force the rights of the community to prevail over the rights of the individual—for instance, with regard to Quranic commandments forbidding drinking or gambling—those and all other ethical issues must constantly be re-evaluated so as to conform to the will of the community.

It must be understood that a respect for human rights, like pluralism, is a process that develops naturally within a democracy. Bear in mind that for years, black American citizens were considered legally inferior to whites. Finally, neither human rights nor pluralism is the result of secularization; they are its root cause. Consequently, any democratic society—Islamic or otherwise—dedicated to the principles of pluralism and human rights must dedicate itself to following the unavoidable path toward political secularization.

Toward a Secularized State

Therein lies the crux of the reformist argument. An Islamic democracy is not intended to be a "theo-democracy," but a democratic system founded upon an Islamic moral framework, devoted to preserving Islamic ideals of pluralism and human rights as they were introduced in Medina, and open to the inevitable process of political secularization. There can be no question as to where sovereignty in such a system would rest. A government of the people, by the people, and for the people can be established or demolished solely through the will of the people. After all, it is human beings who create laws, not God. Even laws based on divine scripture require human interpretation in order to be applied in the world. In any case, sovereignty necessitates the ability not just to make laws but to enforce them. Save for the occasional plague, that is a power God rarely chooses to wield on earth.

That does not mean the religious authorities would have no influence on the state. However, as with the Pope's role in Rome, such influence can be only moral, not political. The function of the clergy in an Islamic democracy is not to rule, but to preserve and, more important, to reflect the morality of the state. Again, because it is not religion but the interpretation of religion that arbitrates morality, such interpretation must always be in accord with the consensus of the community.

From the very moment that God spoke the first word of Revelation to Muhammad—"Recite!"—the story of Islam has been in a constant state of evolution as it responds to the social, cultural, political, and temporal circumstances of those who are telling it. Now it must evolve once more.

It may be too early to know who will write the next chapter of Islam's story, but it is not too early to recognize who will ultimately win the war between reform and counterreform. When 14 centuries ago Muhammad launched a revolution in Mecca to replace the archaic, rigid, and inequitable strictures of tribal society with a radically new vision of divine morality and social egalitarianism, he tore apart the fabric of traditional Arab society. It took many years of violence and devastation to cleanse Arabia of its "false idols." It will take many more to cleanse Islam of its new false idols—bigotry and fanaticism—worshiped by those who have replaced Muhammad's original vision of tolerance and unity with their own ideals of hatred and discord. But the cleansing is inevitable, and the tide of reform cannot be stopped. The Islamic Reformation is already here. We are all living in it.

12

Islam Is Not Compatible with Democracy

David Bukay

David Bukay is a professor of Middle East studies at the University of Haifa, Israel. He is the author of Islamic Fundamentalism and the Arab Political Culture.

The idea that Islam and democracy are compatible has had many champions; however, each proponent has either misunderstood the true requirements of liberal democracy or twisted Islamic ideals to match some Western concepts that are reflections of participatory government. Islam is not compatible with democracy because it does not favor pluralism, and it subordinates personal freedoms to compulsory behaviors based on the will of God. In effect, religious law always takes precedence over human law, ensuring that the people lack sovereignty over their governments and cannot acquire liberties enjoyed in Western democracies.

Are Islam and democracy compatible? A large literature has developed arguing that Islam has all the ingredients of modern state and society. Many Muslim intellectuals seek to prove that Islam enshrines democratic values. But rather than lead the debate, they often follow it, peppering their own analyses with references to Western scholars who, casting aside traditional Orientalism for the theories of the late literary theorist and polemicist Edward Said, twist evidence to fit their theories. Why such efforts? For Western scholars, the answer

David Bukay, "Can There Be an Islamic Democracy?" *Middle East Quarterly*, Spring 2007. Reproduced by permission. www.meforum.org.

lies both in politics and the often lucrative desire to please a wider Middle East audience. For Islamists, though, the motivation is to remove suspicion about the nature and goals of Islamic movements such as the Muslim Brotherhood and, perhaps, even Hezbollah.

Western Supporters of Islamic Democracy

Some Western researchers support the Islamist claim that parliamentary democracy and representative elections are not only compatible with Islamic law, but that Islam actually encourages democracy. They do this in one of two ways: either they twist definitions to make them fit the apparatuses of Islamic government—terms such as democracy become relative—or they bend the reality of life in Muslim countries to fit their theories.

Among the best known advocates of the idea that Islam both is compatible and encourages democracy is John L. Esposito, founding director of the Alwaleed bin Talal Center for Muslim-Christian Understanding at Georgetown University and the author or editor of more than thirty books about Islam and Islamist movements. Esposito and his various co-authors build their arguments upon tendentious assumptions and platitudes such as "democracy has many and varied meanings;" "every culture will mold an independent model of democratic government;" and "there can develop a religious democracy."

He argues that "Islamic movements have internalized the democratic discourse through the concepts of *shura* [consultation], *ijma'* [consensus], and *ijtihad* [independent interpretive judgment]" and concludes that democracy already exists in the Muslim world, "whether the word democracy is used or not."

If Esposito's arguments are true, then why is democracy not readily apparent in the Middle East? [The pro-democracy organization] Freedom House regularly ranks Arab countries as among the least democratic anywhere. Esposito adopts Said's belief that Western scholarship and standards are inherently biased and lambastes both scholars who pass such judgments without experience with Islamic movements and those who have a "secular bias" toward Islam.

[T]he sovereignty of God and sovereignty of the people are mutually exclusive.

For example, in *Islam and Democracy*, Esposito and co-author John Voll, associate director of the Prince Alwaleed Center, question Western attempts to monopolize the definition of democracy and suggest the very concept shifts meanings over time and place. They argue that every culture can mold an independent model of democratic government, which may or may not correlate to the Western liberal idea.

Only after eviscerating the meaning of democracy as the concept developed and derived from Plato and Aristotle in ancient Greece through Thomas Jefferson and James Madison in eighteenth century America, can Esposito and his fellow travelers advance theories of the compatibility of Islamism and democracy.

Examining the Principles of Democracy

While Esposito's arguments may be popular within the Middle East Studies Association, democracy theorists tend to dismiss such relativism. Larry Diamond, co-editor of the *Journal of Democracy*, and Leonardo Morlino, a specialist in comparative politics at the University of Florence, ascribe seven features to any democracy: individual freedoms and civil liberties; rule of the law; sovereignty resting upon the people; equality of all citizens before the law; vertical and horizontal accountability for government officials; transparency of the ruling systems to the demands of the citizens; and equality of opportunity for citizens. This approach is important, since it emphasizes civil liberties, human rights and freedoms, instead of over-reliance on elections and the formal institutions of the state.

Esposito ignores this basic foundation of democracy and instead draws inspiration from men such as Indian philosopher Muhammed Iqbal (1877–1938), Sudanese religious leader Hasan al-Turabi (1932–), Iranian sociologist Ali Shariati (1933–77), and former Iranian president Muhammad Khatami (1943–), who argue that Islam provides a framework for combining democracy with spirituality to remedy the alleged spiritual vacuum in Western democracies. They endorse Khatami's view that democracies need not follow a formula and can function not only in a liberal system but also in socialist or religious systems; they adopt the important twentieth century Indian (and, later, Pakistani) exegete Abu al-A'la al-Mawdudi's concept of a "theo-democracy," in which three principles: *tawhid* (unity of God), *risala* (prophethood) and *khilafa* (caliphate) underlie the Islamic political system.

[M]any Islamists constrain democratic processes and crush civil society. Those with guns, not numbers, shape the state.

But Mawdudi argues that any Islamic polity has to accept the supremacy of Islamic law over all aspects of political and religious life—hardly a democratic concept, given that Islamic law does not provide for equality of all citizens under the law regardless of religion and gender. Such a formulation also denies citizens a basic right to decide their laws, a fundamental concept of democracy. Although he uses the phrase theo-democracy to suggest that Islam encompassed some democratic principles, Mawdudi himself asserted Islamic democracy to be a self-contradiction: the sovereignty of God and sovereignty of the people are mutually exclusive. An Islamic democracy would be the antithesis of secular Western democracy.

Esposito and Voll respond by saying that Mawdudi and his contemporaries did not so much reject democracy as frame it under the concept of God's unity. Theo-democracy need not mean a dictatorship of state, they argue, but rather could include joint sovereignty by all Muslims, including ordinary citizens. Esposito goes even further, arguing that Mawdudi's Islamist system could be democratic even if it eschews popular sovereignty, so long as it permits consultative assemblies subordinate to Islamic law.

While Esposito and Voll argue that Islamic democracy rests upon concepts of consultation (*shura*), consensus (*ijma'*), and independent interpretive judgment (*ijtihad*), other Muslim exegetes add *hakmiya* (sovereignty). To support such a conception of Islamic democracy, Esposito and Voll rely on Muhammad Hamidullah (1908–2002), an Indian Sufi scholar of Islam and international law; Ayatollah Baqir as-Sadr (1935–80), an Iraqi Shi'ite cleric; Muhammad Iqbal (1877–1938), an Indian Muslim poet, philosopher and politician; Khurshid Ahmad, a vice president of the Jama'at-e-lslami of Pakistan; and Taha al-Alwani, an Iraqi scholar of Islamic jurisprudence. The inclusion of Alwani underscores the fallacy of Esposito's theories. In 2003, the FBI identified Alwani as an unindicted co-conspirator in a trial of suspected Palestinian Islamic Jihad leaders and financiers.

Just as Esposito eviscerates the meaning of democracy to enable his thesis, so, too, does he twist Islamic concepts. *Shura* is an advisory council, not a participatory one. It is a legacy of tribalism, not sovereignty. Nor does *ijma'* express the consensus of the community at large but rather only the elders and established leaders. As for independent judgment, many Sunni scholars deem *ijtihad* closed in the eleventh century.

Iranian Reforms Have Not Materialized

Esposito's arguments have not only permeated the Middle Eastern studies academic community but also gained traction with public intellectuals through books written by journalists and policy practitioners.

In both journal articles and book length works as well as in underlying assumptions within her reporting, former *Los Angeles Times* and current *Washington Post* diplomatic correspondent Robin Wright argues that Islamism could transform into more democratic forms. In 2000, for example, she argued in *The Last Great Revolution* that a profound transformation was underway in Iran in which pragmatism replaced revolutionary values, arrogance had given way to realism, and the "government of God" was ceding to secular statecraft. Far from becoming more democratic, though, the supreme leader and Revolutionary Guards consolidated control; freedoms remain elusive, political prisoners incarcerated, and democracy imaginary.

Underlying Wright's work is the idea that neither Islam nor Muslim culture is a major obstacle to political modernity. She accepts both the Esposito school's arguments that *shura*, *ijma'*, and *ijtihad* form a basis on which to make Islam compatible with political pluralism. She shares John Voll's belief that Islam is an integral part of the modern world, and she says the central drama of reform is the attempt to reconcile Islam and modernity by creating a worldview compatible with both.

In her article "Islam and Liberal Democracy," she profiles two prominent Islamist thinkers, Rachid al-Ghannouchi, the exiled leader of Tunisia's Hizb al-Nahda (Renaissance Party), and Iranian philosopher and analytical chemist Abdul-Karim Soroush. While she argues that their ideas represent a realistic confluence of Islam and democracy, she neither defines democracy nor treats her case studies with a dispassionate eye. Ghannouchi uses democratic terms without accepting them let alone understanding their meaning. He remains not a modernist but an unapologetic Islamist.

Wright ignores that Soroush led the purge of liberal intellectuals from Iranian universities in the wake of the Islamic Revolution. While Soroush spoke of civil rights and tolerance, he applied such privileges only to those subscribing to Islamic democracy. He also argued that although Islam means "submission," there is no contradiction to the freedoms inherent in democracy. Islam and democracy are not only compatible but their association inevitable. In a Muslim society, one without the other is imperfect. He argues that the will of the majority shapes the ideal Islamic state. But, in practice, this does not occur. As in Iran, many Islamists constrain democratic processes and crush civil society. Those with guns, not numbers, shape the state. Among Arab-Islamic states, there are only authoritarian regimes and patrimonial leadership; the jury is still out on whether Iraq can be a stable exception. Soroush, however, contradicts himself: Although Islam should be an open religion, it must retain its essence. His argument that Islamic law is expandable would be considered blasphemous by many contemporaries who argue that certain principles within Islamic law are immutable. Upon falling out of favor with revolutionary authorities in Iran, he fled to the West. Sometimes, academics only face the fallacy of what sounds plausible in the ivy tower when events force them to face reality.

[W]hile Western scholars perform intellectual somersaults to demonstrate the compatibility of Islam and democracy, prominent Muslim scholars argue democracy to be incompatible with their religion.

What Ghannouchi and Soroush have in common, and what remains true with any number of other Islamist officials, is that, regardless of rhetoric, they do not wish to reconcile Islam and modernity but to change the political order. It is easier to adopt the rhetoric of democracy than its principles. . . .

Other scholars take obsequiousness to new levels. Anna Jordan, who gives no information about her expertise but is widely published on Islamist Internet sites, argues that the Qur'an supports the principles of Western democracy as they are defined by William Ebenstein and Edwin Fogelman, two professors of political science who focus on the ideas and ideologies that define democracy. By utilizing various Qur'anic verses, Jordan finds that the Islamic holy book supports rational empiricism and individual rights, rejects the state as the ultimate authority, promotes the freedom to associate with any religious group, accepts the idea that the state is subordinate to law, and accepts due process and basic equality.

Most of her citations, though, do not support her conclusions and, in some cases, suggest the opposite. Rather than support the idea of "rational empiricism," for example, Sura 17:36 mandates complete submission to the authority of God. Other citations are irrelevant in context and substance to her arguments. Her assertion that the Qur'an assures the "basic equality of all human beings" rests upon verses commanding equality among Muslims and Muslims only, plus a verse warning against schisms among Muslims.

Gudrun Kramer, chair of the Institute of Islamic Studies at the Free University in Berlin, also accepts the Esposito thesis. She writes that the central stream in Islam "has come to accept crucial elements of political democracy: pluralism, political participation, governmental accountability, the rule of law, and the protection of human rights." In her opinion, the Muslim approach to human rights and freedom is more advanced than many Westerners acknowledge.

Islamist Thinkers Reject Democracy

Ironically, while Western scholars perform intellectual somersaults to demonstrate the compatibility of Islam and democracy, prominent Muslim scholars argue democracy to be incompatible with their religion. They base their conclusion on two foundations: first, the conviction that Islamic law regulates the believer's activities in every area of life, and second, that the Muslim society of believers will attain all its goals only if the believers walk in the path of God. In addition, some Muslim scholars further reject anything that does not have its origins in the Qur'an.

The Islamic world is not ready to absorb the basic values of modernism and democracy.

Hasan al-Banna (1906–49), the founder of the Muslim Brotherhood, sought to purge Western influences. He taught that Islam was the only solution and that democracy amounted to infidelity to Islam. Sayyid Qutb (1906–66), the leading theoretician of the Muslim Brotherhood, objected to the idea of popular sovereignty altogether. He believed that the Islamic state must be based upon the Qur'an, which he argued provided a complete and moral system in need of no further legislation. Consultation—in the traditional Islamic sense rather than in the manner of Esposito's extrapolations—was sufficient.

Mawdudi, while used by Esposito, argued that Islam was the antithesis of any secular Western democracy that based sovereignty upon the people and rejected the basics of Western democracy. More recent Islamists such as Qaradawi argue that democracy must be subordinate to the acceptance of God as the basis of sovereignty. Democratic elections are therefore heresy, and since religion makes law, there is no need for legislative bodies. Outlining his plans to establish an Islamic state in Indonesia, Abu Bakar Bashir, a Muslim cleric and the leader of the Indonesian Mujahideen Council, attacked democracy and the West and called on Muslims to wage jihad against the ruling regimes in the Muslim world. "It is not democracy that we want, but Allah-cracy," he explained.

Nor does acceptance of basic Western structures imply democracy. Under Ayatollah Ruhollah Khomeini, the Islamic Republic adopted both a constitution and a parliament, but their existence did not make Iran more democratic. Indeed, Khomeini continued to wield supreme power and formed a number of bodies—the revolutionary foundations, for example—which remained above constitutional law.

The Islamic World Is Not Ready for Democracy

The Islamic world is not ready to absorb the basic values of modernism and democracy. Leadership remains the prerogative of the ruling elite. Arab and Islamic leadership are patrimonial, coercive, and authoritarian. Such basic principles as sovereignty, legitimacy, political participation and pluralism, and those individual rights and freedoms inherent in democracy do not exist in a system where Islam is the ultimate source of law.

Islamists themselves regard liberal democracy with contempt. They are willing to accommodate it as an avenue to power but as an avenue that runs only one way.

The failure of democracies to take hold in Gaza and Iraq justify both the 1984 declaration by Samuel P. Huntington [author of *Clash of Civilizations and the Remaking of World Order*] and the argument a decade later by Gilles Kepel, a prominent French scholar and analyst of radical Islam, that Islamic cultural traditions may prevent democratic development.

Emeritus Princeton historian Bernard Lewis is also correct in explaining that the term democracy is often misused. It has turned up in surprising places—the Spain of General Franco, the Greece of the colonels, the Pakistan of the generals, the Eastern Europe of the commissars—usually prefaced by some qualifying adjective such as "guided," "basic," "organic," "popular," or the like, which serves to dilute, deflect, or even reverse the meaning of the word.

Islam may be compatible with democracy, but it depends on what is understood as Islam. This is not universally agreed on and is based on a hope, not on reality. Both Turkey and the West African country of Mali are democracies even though the vast majority of their citizens are Muslim. But, the political Islam espoused by the Muslim Brotherhood and other Islamists is incompatible with liberal democracy.

Furthermore, if language has an impact on thinking, then the Middle East will achieve democracy only slowly, if at all. In traditional Arabic, Persian, and Turkish, there is no word for "citizen." Rather, older texts use cognates—in Arabic, *muwatin*; in Turkish, *vatandaslik*; in Persian, *sharunad*—respectively, closer in meaning to the English "compatriot" or "countryman." The Arabic and Turkish come from *watan*, meaning "country." *Muwatin*, is a neologism and while it suggests progress, the Western concept of freedom—understood as the ability to participate in the formation, conduct, and lawful removal and replacement of government—remains alien in much of the region.

Islamists themselves regard liberal democracy with contempt. They are willing to accommodate it as an avenue to power but as an avenue that runs only one way. Hisham Sharabi (1927–2005), the influential Palestinian scholar and political activist, has said that Islamic fundamentalism expresses mass sentiment and belief as no nationalist or socialist (and we may add democratic) ideology has been able to do up until now.

Political Correctness and Propaganda

Why then are so many Western scholars keen to show the compatibility between Islamism and democracy? The popularity of post-colonialism and post-modernism within the academy inclines intellectuals to accommodate Islamism. Political correctness inhibits many from addressing the negative phenomenon in foreign cultures. It is considered laudable to prove the compatibility of Islam and democracy; it is labeled "Islamophobic" or racist to suggest incompatibility or to differentiate between positive and negative interpretations of Islam.

Many policymakers are also conflict-adverse. Islamists exploit the Western cultural desire to accommodate while Western thinkers and policymakers attempt to ameliorate differences by seeking to find common ground in definitions if not reality.

Into the mix comes Islamist propaganda, portraying Islam as peace-loving, embracing of civil rights and, even in its less tolerant forms, compatible with all democratic values. The problem is that the free world ignores the possibility that political Islam can threaten democracy not only in Middle Eastern societies but also in the West. The legitimization of political Islam has lent democratic respectability to an ideology and political system at odds with the basic tenets of democracy.

Esposito's statement that "the United States must restrain its one-dimensional attitude to democracy and recognize [that] the authentic roots of democracy exist in Islam" shows a basic ignorance of both democracy and Islamist teachings. These conclusions are exacerbated when Esposito places blame for the aggressiveness and terrorism of Islamic fundamentalism on the West and on Said's "Orientalists." It is one thing to be wrong in the classroom, but it can be far more dangerous when such wrong-headed theories begin to affect policy.

Organizations to Contact

The editors have compiled the following list of organizations concerned with the issues debated in this book. The descriptions are derived from materials provided by the organizations. All have publications or information available for interested readers. The list was compiled on the date of publication of the present volume; the information provided here may change. Be aware that many organizations take several weeks or longer to respond to inquiries, so allow as much time as possible.

America-Mideast Educational and Training Services
1730 M St. NW, Suite 1100, Washington, DC   20036-4505
(202) 776-9600 • fax: (202) 776-7000
e-mail: inquiries@amideast.org
Web site: www.amideast.org

AMIDEAST promotes understanding and cooperation between Americans and the people of the Middle East and North Africa through education and development programs. It publishes the *AMIDEAST Today* newsletter, and various press releases are available on the organization's Web site.

American-Arab Anti-Discrimination Committee
1732 Wisconsin Ave, NW, Washington, DC   20007
(202) 244-2990 • fax: (202) 244-7968
e-mail: ADC@adc.org
Web site: www.adc.org

ADC is a grassroots organization that supports Arab-American rights and encourages Arab-American participation in American society. It also fights discrimination and hate crimes against Arab Americans. It publishes a series of issue papers and a number of books that can be ordered from its online store.

American Muslim Council
1005 W. Webster, Suite #3, Chicago, IL 60614
(773) 248-3390
e-mail: info@amcnational.org
Web site: www.amcnational.org

AMC is a nonprofit organization established to identify and oppose discrimination against Muslims and other minorities and to raise the level of social awareness and political involvement of Muslims in the United States. It publishes the monthly newsletter *AMC Report* and numerous pamphlets and monographs.

Arab World and Islamic Resources
P.O. Box 174, Abiquiu, NM 87510
(510) 704-0517
e-mail: awair@igc.apc.org
Web site: www.awaironline.org

AWAIR provides materials and services for educators teaching about the Arab world and about Islam at the precollege level. It publishes many books and videos on Arab history, current events, and other Arab studies.

Council of American-Islamic Relations
453 New Jersey Ave. SE, Washington, DC 20003
(202) 488-8787 • fax: (202) 488-0833
e-mail: info@cair.com
Web site: www.cair-net.org

CAIR is an advocacy group devoted to protecting the rights of Arab-Americans and promoting a positive image of Islam in the United States. The CAIR Web site offers many press releases and position papers on current events, and it details its outreach programs to facilitate a greater understanding of Islam. The site also provides primers for Arab-Americans who are concerned about possible civil rights violations.

International Institute of Islamic Thought
500 Grove Street, Herndon, VA   20170
(703) 471-1133 • fax: (703) 471-3922
e-mail: iiit@iiit.org
Web site: www.iiit.org

IIIT is a nonprofit academic research facility that promotes and coordinates research and related activities in Islamic philosophy, the humanities, and social sciences. It publishes numerous books in both Arabic and English as well as the quarterly *American Journal of Islamic Social Science* and the *Muslim World Book Review*.

Islamic Circle of North America
166-26 89th Ave., Jamaica, NY   11432
(718) 658-1199 • fax: (718) 658-1255
e-mail: info@icna.org
Web site: www.icna.org

ICNA is an Islamic support organization that seeks to promote the values and duties of the Islamic religion. It maintains a charitable relief organization and publishes numerous pamphlets in its *Islamic Da 'wah* series as well as the monthly magazine, the *Message*. Its Web site offers downloads and podcasts relating to Islamic teachings.

Islamic Information Center of America
Box 4052, Des Plaines, IL   60016
e-mail: iica1@comcast.net
Web site: www.iica.org

IICA is a nonprofit organization that provides information about Islam to Muslims, the general public, and the media. It publishes and distributes a number of pamphlets and a monthly newsletter, the *Invitation*.

Islamic Texts Society
22A Brooklands Ave., Cambridge   CB2 2DQ
  UK
+44 (0) 1223 31487 • fax: +44 (0) 1223 324342

e-mail: mail@its.org.uk
Web site: www.its.org.uk

The Islamic Texts Society publishes and sells English transla-
tions of works of importance to the faith and culture of Islam, with the aim of promoting a greater understanding of Islam. Among the titles it offers are *Islam and the Plight of
Modern Man* and *The History and the Philosophy of Islamic
Science.*

Middle East Institute

1761 N St. NW, Washington, DC   20036-2882
(202) 785-1141 • fax: (202) 331-8861
e-mail: mideasti@mideasti.org
Web site: www.themiddleeastinstitute.org

The Middle East Institute's mission is to promote a better understanding of Middle Eastern cultures, languages, religions,
and politics. It publishes numerous books, papers, audiotapes,
and videos as well as the quarterly *Middle East Journal*. It also
maintains an Educational Outreach Department to give teach-
ers and students of all grade levels advice on resources.

Middle East Outreach Council

Portland State University, Portland, OR   97207-0751
(503) 725-8566
e-mail: campbej@pdx.edu
Web site: www.meoc.us

MEOC is a nonprofit, nonpolitical organization that seeks to
increase public knowledge about the lands, cultures, and
peoples of the Middle East through workshops, seminars, and
educational materials. It publishes the *Middle East Outreach
Council Newsletter* three times a year.

Middle East Policy Council (MEPC)

1730 M St. NW, Suite 512, Washington, DC   20036
(202) 296-6767 • fax: (202) 296-5791

e-mail: info@mepc.org
Web site: www.mepc.org

The purpose of MEPC is to facilitate an understanding of current issues regarding U.S. relations with Middle Eastern countries. It publishes the quarterly journal *Middle East Policy* as well as special reports and books. The MEPC Web site offers suggested readings on various topics in Middle Eastern affairs.

Middle East Research and Information Project
1500 Massachusetts Ave. NW, Suite 199
Washington, DC   20005
(202) 223-3677 • fax: (202) 223-3604
Web site: www.merip.org

MERIP's mission is to educate the public about the contemporary Middle East, with particular emphasis on U.S. policy, human rights, and social justice issues. It publishes the bimonthly *Middle East Report.*

Middle East Studies Association
University of Arizona, Tucson, AZ   85721
(520) 621-5850 • fax: (520) 626-9095
e-mail: mesana@u.arizona.edu
Web site: www.mesana.org

The Middle East Studies Association is an academic collective of scholars on the Middle East. It publishes bulletins, a newsletter, and the quarterly *International Journal of Middle East Studies* and reviews textbooks that cover the Middle East.

Muslim Public Affairs Council
3010 Wilshire Blvd., Suite 217, Los Angeles, CA   90010
(213) 383-3443 • fax: (213) 383-9674
e-mail: mpac-contact@mpac.org
Web site: www.mpac.org

MPAC is a nonprofit, public services agency that strives to disseminate accurate information about Muslims and achieve cooperation between various communities on the basis of shared values such as peace, justice, freedom, and dignity. It publishes and distributes a number of reports on issues of concern to the Muslim community, such as U.S. foreign relations and human rights policy. It also publishes a newsletter under the title *Impact*.

Washington Institute for Near East Policy
1828 L St. NW, Washington, DC   20036
(202) 452-0650 • fax: (202) 223-5364
e-mail: info@washingtoninstitute.org
Web site: www.washingtoninstitute.org

The Washington Institute for Near East Policy is an independent, nonprofit research organization that provides information and analysis on the Middle East and U.S. policy in the region. It publishes numerous books, periodic monographs, and reports on regional politics, security, and economics, including *Operation Iraqi Freedom and the New Iraq* and *The Battle of Ideas in the War on Terror*.

Bibliography

Books

Charles Allen — *God's Terrorists: The Wahhabi Cult and Hidden Roots of Modern Jihad.* New York: Little, Brown, 2006.

Bruce Bawer — *While Europe Slept: How Radical Islam is Destroying the West from Within.* New York: Doubleday, 2006.

David Cook — *Martyrdom in Islam.* New York: Cambridge University Press, 2007.

David Cook — *Understanding Jihad.* Berkeley: University of California Press, 2005.

Nonie Darwish — *Now They Call Me Infidel: Why I Renounced Jihad for America, Israel, and the War on Terror.* New York: Penguin, 2006.

Meghnad Desai — *Rethinking Islamism: The Ideology of the New Terror.* New York: I. B. Tauris, 2007.

Timothy R. Furnish — *Holiest Wars: Islamic Mahdis, Their Jihads, and Osama bin Laden.* Westport, CT: Praeger, 2005.

Fawaz A. Gerges — *Journey of the Jihadist: Inside Muslim Militancy.* New York: Harcourt, 2006.

Samuel P. Huntington — *The Clash of Civilizations and the Remaking of World Order.* New York: Simon & Schuster, 1998.

Joseph E. B. Lumbard, ed. *Islam, Fundamentalism, and the Betrayal of Tradition: Essays by Western Muslim Scholars.* Bloomington, IN: World Wisdom, 2004.

Terry McDermott *Perfect Soldiers: The Hijackers: Who They Were, Why They Did It.* New York: HarperCollins, 2005.

George Michael *The Enemy of My Enemy: The Alarming Convergence of Militant Islam and the Extreme Right.* Lawrence, KS: University Press of Kansas, 2006.

Beverley Milton-Edwards *Islamic Fundamentalism since 1945.* New York: Routledge, 2005.

Angel M. Rabasa, et al. *The Muslim World after 9/11.* Santa Monica, CA: RAND, 2004.

Kevin J. Ryan *Radical Eye for the Infidel Guy: Inside the Strange World of Militant Islam.* Amherst, NY: Prometheus, Books, 2007.

Robert Spencer *Onward Muslim Soldiers: How Jihad Still Threatens America and the West.* Washington, DC: Regnery, 2003.

Bassam Tibi *The Challenge of Fundamentalism: Political Islam and the New World Disorder.* Berkeley: University of California Press, 2002.

Lorenzo Vidino *Al Qaeda in Europe: The New Battleground of International Jihad.* Amherst, NY: Prometheus Books, 2006.

Periodicals

David Aikman   "Garlic, Dracula, and Al Qaeda,"
                    Christianity Today, December, 2006.

Atlantic Monthly "The Phantom Menace," July/August,
                    2006.

Tony Blair   "Dealing With the Middle East," *Vital
                    Speeches of the Day*, October 1, 2006.

George W. Bush   "Global War on Terror," *Vital
                    Speeches of the Day*, October 1, 2006.

Dinesh D'Souza   "Radical Islam: We Harm Ourselves
                    by Not Understanding What Drives
                    Terrorists," *San Diego Union-Tribune*,
                    February 4, 2007.

Economist   "School for Terror," August 8, 2006.

Mariam Fam   "'Brotherhood' Blogs in Egypt Offer
                    View of Young Islamists," *Wall Street
                    Journal, Eastern Edition*, April 20,
                    2007.

Hassan M. Fattah,   "Bickering Saudis Struggle for an
et al.   Answer to Iran's Rising Influence in
                    the Middle East," *New York Times*,
                    December 12, 2006.

Jeffrey Gettleman   "Demonstrations Become Clashes
                    after Islamists Take Somali City," *New
                    York Times*, September 26, 2006.

Jeffrey Gettleman   "Islamists Held Trying to Flee From
                    Somalia into Kenya," *New York Times*,
                    January 18, 2007.

Paul Jeffrey — "Religious Aftershock," *Christian Century*, September 9, 2006.

Adnan R. Khan — "Words That Can Kill," *Maclean's*, January 1, 2007.

Charles Krauthammer — "Actually, the Middle East Is Our Crisis Too," *Time*, August 7, 2006.

Michael Luo — "On Dangerous Footing in Iraq, Where Dancing Is a Courageous Act," *New York Times*, October 30, 2006.

Sarah Lyall — "Hungry for Fresh Recruits, Cult-Like *Islamic* Groups Know Just When to Pounce," *New York Times*, August 8, 2006.

Joshua Micah Marshall — "Practice to Deceive: Chaos in the Middle East Is Not the Bush Hawks' Nightmare Scenario—It's Their Plan," *Washington Monthly*, April 2003.

David Meir-Levi — "Terrorism: The Root Causes," *Front Page Magazine*, November 9, 2005. www.frontpagemag.com.

National Review — "Guests of the Ayatollah: The First Battle in America's War with Militant Islam," August 7, 2006.

Asra Q. Nomani — "A Daring Voice Calls For a New Islam," *Time*, May 8, 2006.

Michael Petrou — "The Scariest Man on Earth," *Maclean's*, January 23, 2006.

| Chitra Ragavan | "A Troubling Sense of Déjà Vu," *U.S. News & World Report*, July 24, 2006. |

| Charley Reese | "Islamic Democrats," *Washington Report on Middle East Affairs*, September 2004. |

| William Safire | "Islamofascism," *New York Times Magazine*, October 1, 2006. |

| Elaine Sciolino | "Teacher in Hiding after Attack on Islam Stirs Threats," *New York Times*, September 30, 2006. |

| Roger Scruton | "'Islamofascism': Beware of a Religion without Irony," *Wall Street Journal*, August 20, 2006. |

| Martin Slann | "Hatred of the West," *Chronicle of Higher Education*, April 21, 2006. |

| Khaled Abu Toameh | "Radical Chic," *U.S. News & World Report*, February 13, 2006. |

| Alex Tresniowski, et al. | "The Bomber Next Door," *People*, August 28, 2006. |

| *USA Today* | "Bush, bin Laden Visit Pakistan in Tellingly Different Ways," March 3, 2006. |

| Mortimer B. Zuckerman | "The Threat from Within," *U.S. News & World Report*, December 18, 2006. |

Index

Wright, Robin, 66, 105–106

Z

Zafar, Ibn, 15
al-Zawahiri, Ayman, 65

Zunes, Stephen, 32, 36, 37